Y0-BCR-476

THE FRENCH WARS OF RELIGION

How Important Were Religious Factors?

THE FRENCH WARS OF RELIGION

How Important Were Religious Factors?

EDITED WITH AN INTRODUCTION BY

J. H. M. Salmon

UNIVERSITY OF WAIKATO, NEW ZEALAND

D. C. HEATH AND COMPANY • BOSTON

Library of Congress Catalog Card Number 67-25414

Printed August, 1967

Table of Contents

Introduction

FOR FOUR DECADES after the accidental death of the Valois King, Henry II, in 1559, France was convulsed by anarchy and civil war. Armed conflict began with the abortive conspiracy of Amboise in 1560, and erupted into open warfare in 1562. It continued, with some early intervals, until the first Bourbon, Henry IV, made peace with his Catholic enemies and granted toleration to French Protestantism in 1598. During this period the monarchy, which had achieved the territorial unity of France in the fifteenth century and had subsequently defied the encircling Hapsburg powers of Spain and the Empire, was reduced to a nullity. In the reigns of Francis II, Charles IX, and Henry III, it became the plaything of contending aristocratic factions and proved incapable of imposing that middle course between the religious parties which the Queen Mother, Catherine de Medici, pursued at the commencement of the struggle. The eclipse of the central government and the bureaucratic agencies it had fostered was accompanied by the reassertion of old centrifugal tendencies. Endemic local disorder was magnified by religious disturbances. As the wars intensified, the disruption of commercial life and the devastations of undisciplined armies provoked a swelling torrent of discontent, which spilled over into popular risings within the cities and among the peasantry.

The French time of troubles should be seen in a context wider than that of internal anarchy. The intimate connections between revolt in France and in the Netherlands suggest the larger aspect of the conflict. There is a sense in which France in the second half of the sixteenth century became, like Germany in the Thirty Years' War, a European battleground for the supranational struggle of Reformation and Counter-Reformation. Mercenary or national contingents from Germany, Spain, England, and Italy were numbered among the forces of the combatants. The very origin of the wars was linked with international dynastic and religious problems. The earlier political repercussions of Protestantism in Germany placed the French monarchy in a dilemma. Since the Emperor Charles V had set his face against the Reformation, Henry II had eventually to choose between his religious and diplomatic interests. While it was necessary for the Valois to make allies of the German Protestant princes if the wars against the Hapsburgs were to be continued, this anti-Catholic foreign policy was incompatible with the traditional orthodoxy of the French crown and its repression of Protestantism at home. Although it was by no means the sole reason for civil war, Henry II's decision in 1559 to make peace with Spain and to cooperate with Philip II against the Protestant cause foreshadowed the internal conflict.

The reign of Henry II was marked by the rivalry of the two great aristocratic houses of Montmorency and Guise. When the Guises secured the ascendancy after the King's death, they identified themselves with the ultra-Catholic cause. Early French Protestantism had generally been Lutheran in outlook, though it embodied elements derived from native inspiration.[1] From the middle 1550's, however, the movement was organised and extended by Calvinist missionaries and closely linked with Geneva. Calvinism found a ready following among the lesser nobility who,

[1] M. Lucien Febvre has demonstrated the futility of the long-standing dispute as to whether French Protestantism should be seen as a foreign intrusion or as a movement rooted in the French genius: *Au Coeur religieux du XVIe siècle,* Paris 1957, pp. 3–70.

moved by anti-clerical designs on the wealth of the church and deprived of their habitual occupation of foreign war, became a militant threat to Guisard supremacy. Leadership came not from the house of Montmorency, which, with the exception of Admiral Coligny and his brothers, remained loyal to the orthodox faith, but rather from the house of Bourbon, itself related to the royal line. When the Queen Mother's attempts at balancing the factions broke down, the Huguenots embarked upon the two civil wars of 1562–63 and 1567–68 under the banner of the Bourbon prince, Louis de Condé. At Condé's death in 1569 during the third war, Coligny assumed the direction of Huguenot strategy and forced the monarchy to come to terms in the following year. The Admiral won the confidence of Charles IX, the brother and successor to Francis II, and persuaded the King to support Protestant resistance to Spain in the Netherlands. This reversion to the traditional foreign policy might have attracted the anti-Hapsburg sympathies of the Queen Mother, had she not distrusted Coligny's haste to begin hostilities and resented his ascendancy over her son. Her attempt to eliminate the Huguenot leader by assassination led, through miscalculation and the unleashing of the fanaticism of Catholic Paris, to the slaughter of the Protestants on St. Bartholomew's Day 1572.

After the Massacre, French Protestantism reshaped both its political ideals and its organization, and continued to defend its independent status in the wars which followed the accession of Henry III in 1574. But when Anjou, the youngest of Catherine de Medici's four sons, died in 1584 and the Protestant Bourbon, Henry of Navarre, became heir presumptive to the throne, many Huguenots proved ready to aid the moderate Catholic faction and to support the principles of hereditary monarchy. It was then the turn of the Catholic League to oppose the Crown. The reaction to the Massacre of St. Bartholomew, and the leadership provided by the Montmorency family, had created a middle party, known as the *Politiques,* which subordinated the need for Catholic uniformity to political considerations. The League first became a coherent political organization in its resistance to the *politique* peace negotiated with the Huguenots in 1576. In 1584 it was revived in a yet more militant form to deny recognition to Navarre. Led by Henry of Guise, it entered into close association with Spain. Despite its aristocratic headship, the League employed the lower clergy as its organ of propaganda, and within the capital assumed the guise of a popular conspiracy under an inner ring of revolutionaries known as "the Sixteen." Henry III strove to create a third force about the throne, but his powerful favorites, especially the Dukes of Epernon and Joyeuse, leaned either to Navarre or to Guise, and the continuing wars favored the extremist groups at the expense of the monarchy. In May 1588, the King fled from Paris to escape a popular demonstration supporting Henry of Guise, and soon afterwards he accepted the complete domination of the League. But before the end of the year he turned on his oppressors and had Guise murdered during an assembly of the representative Estates General at Blois. The League then threw off its nominal allegiance to the last Valois, and recognized Guise's brother, Mayenne, as the custodian of the authority of the crown. Henry III was obliged to ally himself with Navarre, and in July 1589 their joint armies were advancing on Paris when the King was struck down by the knife of a Leaguer assassin.

Although the League was handicapped by the disparate nature of the elements that composed it, nine further years of warfare and negotiation were needed before Henry IV won general recognition of his authority. He did not secure Paris until he had abjured his Protestant faith, and his conversion cost him the support of the Huguenot movement. French Protestant contingents withdrew from the open war with Spain declared in 1595. The Edict of Nantes guaranteeing their liberties was extracted from the monarchy three years later by the obdurate bargaining of their leaders. In every province and major town rival authorities disputed the possession of power and often pursued local rather than national objectives. Gradually the Leaguer aristocracy were divided from their cause, and the republican independence of the towns was undermined. The King defeated his enemies with the support of the *Politiques,* who came to profess a belief in the absolute power of monarchy by Divine Right. Both the Huguenots and the Catholic League had in turn developed theories, first of constitutional restraints upon the crown and then of the abstract right of the nation to discipline or depose its ruler. Like the Estates General, which had played an important role in several crucial phases of the wars, these theories were to be superseded by the power and prestige of the Bourbon monarchy. The crown alone seemed capable of healing the wounds inflicted by the last and most intensive phase of the Wars of Religion.

So bare a summary of events conceals a number of problems which have excited controversy among historians. The intermingling of political and religious motives in a context of economic instability and rapid social change has suggested a variety of interpretations of the principal causes and essential characteristics of the conflict. While it may be acknowledged that the climate of sixteenth-century opinion reduced politics to a branch of theology, from the sceptical Montaigne to the modern historian there has always been a compulsion to distinguish secular from spiritual aspirations. Protestant writers, such as Samuel Mours and Emile Léonard, see Huguenot resistance largely in terms of a justifiable response to persecution. The work of Robert Kingdon, however, reveals a note of aggression from the Genevan pastors in the preparation and conduct of armed revolt. Dr. Sutherland, in her study of the Conspiracy of Amboise of 1560, has investigated the connection between the Protestant movement, the growth of a political opposition, and the origins of the civil wars. Calvin is shown to have played an indecisive role because his lofty idealism bore no relation to political realities. In failing to offer his followers any practical solution to material problems, he lost control of the Protestant movement in France. Other historians describe the Huguenots as the instigators of the wars and regard their religious propaganda as a cloak for political ambition. James Westfall Thompson accepts this conclusion but distinguishes between "religious Huguenots," who strove to convert all France to their beliefs, and "political Huguenots," whose energies were directed against the crown.

These analyses of the entwining of religious and political motives are set against the background of disorder accompanying the collapse or decay of the institutions of church and state. An additional insight into this background is provided by the social aspects considered by Henri Hauser and, to a less extent, by Lucien Romier. French Protestantism is held to have experienced a sudden change in direction after its capture by the lesser nobility. This class is depicted as impoverished by rising inflation and unable to alter the fixed landed rents upon which their incomes were based. Greed for court favors and church land and a readiness to repair fortunes by banditry and war are seen as principal elements in Huguenot aggression. Such considerations are again mentioned in Sir John Neale's survey of the origins of the wars, but they are not given as large a place as are the financial repercussions of the foreign wars of the preceding period. The bankruptcy of the government, the burden of taxation, and the breakdown of the fiscal machine are seen as important reasons for the reaction against the administration of the Guises. When the wavering policies of Catherine de Medici replace their conduct of affairs, her blunders and miscalculations serve to turn widespread discontent into civil war.

The Wars of Religion were so protracted in their course, and underwent such striking changes of direction, that generalizations about their causes do not always explain their essential nature. Many historians draw sharp distinctions between the character of Protestant resistance and that of the revolt of the Catholic League. In the romantic vision of Jules Michelet, however, the whole period has a thematic unity. It becomes a conflict between the incipient forces of patriotic democracy and those of a foreign and reactionary Catholicism. The Huguenots form part of an international Protestant crusade to preserve liberty and intellectual progress. Despite their aristocratic leadership, they are the anticipators of French republicanism. In contrast, the League becomes a sinister conspiracy to destroy the unity of France and prostrate it before external enemies. Manifestations of Leaguer fanaticism are discerned at the very onset of civil strife; its democratic elements are branded as "a priest-led rabble."

The older tradition of Protestant historiography, like Michelet's interpretation, has denigrated the League. It has also condemned the policy of the Catholic monarchy, and depicted it as Machiavellian, in the once common pejorative sense of the word. The reaction against this view receives its strongest expression in Jean Héritier's biography of Catherine de Medici. M. Héritier sees the wars as a struggle between the forces of anarchy, whether Protestant or Catholic, and the sense of national unity represented by the crown and personified in the Queen Mother. Catherine is Machiavellian in the more fashionable sense, that is, as a realistic defender of the national interest, whose guiding principle is Reason of State. Such opinions are most evident in Héritier's account of the Massacre of St. Bartholomew — an event which in itself was for long the centre of historical controversy.

One of the interpretations of the Massacre, which was employed in the early nineteenth century to replace the view that the slaughter had been long premeditated by the crown, was the theory of an explosion of mob fanaticism. Héritier and other modern writers on the Massacre admit this as one factor among many and see the actions of the Parisian lower classes in 1572 as a prologue to the League. To Michelet's contemporary, Jean-Baptiste Capefigue, the direct assertion of the popular will is a prevailing characteristic of the Wars of Religion. The appearance of Parisian Catholic democracy at critical moments in the conflicts suggests to him that it is a determining influence. For Capefigue the crowd scenes of the Parisian League are anticipations of the Revolution of 1789. The triumph of democratic Catholicism revives the spirit of municipal independence. The clergy are the tribunate of the people. A generation after Capefigue, Paul Robiquet specifically denies a parallel between the Wars of Religion and the Revolution. In his study of the role of the Parisian League, Robiquet affirms that in this phase of the wars, as in every other, the nature of the struggle was essentially aristocratic. The family of Guise is seen as dominating the League, and its members are held to have repudiated popular principles, and to have controlled or repressed the tumultuous assemblies of the Parisian lower orders.

It is to be expected that those who discern in the Wars of Religion political forces of continuing relevance to the France of their own day should neglect the international aspects of the conflict. In contrast, De Lamar Jensen's recent study of relations between Spain and the League finds a key to the nature of the wars in their wider, European context. The Catholic interests of Philip II, expressed through the role of his ambassador, Bernadino de Mendoza, in the counsels of the League, exercise a controlling influence over the development of events in France. The popular Catholic elements retain their importance, for it is through these, rather than through the self-seeking Leaguer princes, that Spanish and Catholic aims are pursued by Mendoza. Jensen maintains that Spanish policies were responsible for exacerbating the divisions within the League, and thus for the ultimate defeat of supranational religious ideals.

A belief that the nature of the wars can be better distinguished by provincial studies than by the search for a broad political pattern has influenced a number of modern historians. The clash of national and local interests is demonstrated in Henri Drouot's account of Mayenne's dual role as leader of the League and would-be sovereign of the province of Burgundy. Like many of his associates among the princes, Mayenne built up his provincial independence and endeavored to check the yet more localized ambitions of his clientèle within the towns and among the nobility. But his dream of establishing a new Burgundian dynasty proved incompatible with the need to maintain those centralized monarchical institutions he needed to maintain his party on a national basis. Separatism becomes the essential characteristic of the Wars of Religion. This aspect of Drouot's study of Burgundy has not been represented by a selection in this volume; but the same centrifugal trend is analyzed in an extract from the work of Fernand Braudel, who has described the civil wars in Provence as a part of his general study of Mediterranean civilization in the sixteenth century. Important as were the bewildering local conflicts of the Provençal nobility, the struggles between rival governors and the intervention of Savoy and Spain, to Braudel the most significant of all the forces of division is the revival of municipal independence and the creation of such city-republics as Marseille.

Opinions on the principal consequences of the Wars of Religion are nearly as diverse as those upon their nature. It has been argued that the French *crise de conscience* produced a mold for liberal political principles which was to form later European ideas. It has also been maintained that the triumph of absolute monarchy caused such subversive doctrines to be speedily forgotten. In his chapters on France at the conclusion of the wars, M. Mariéjol stresses the impotence and lack of prestige of the central government. The general impression is one of universal devastation and the breakdown of constituted authority. Every group in French society, save that of the magistrature, is depicted as utterly demoralized. Pierre de Vaissière is more selective, and designates the rural nobility as the principal victim. He denies the claims examined earlier that this class was impoverished by the price rise in the first half of the century and that their impoverishment is among the causes of the wars. On the contrary, the earlier period is declared to be the golden age of the nobility, and the civil wars are held to have uprooted them from their rural environment and ultimately to have facilitated their enslavement by the crown. Economic ruin of noble fortunes is the consequence, not the cause, of the Wars of Religion. Henri Drouot extends this interpretation and relates it more directly to the evidence. He regards the plight of the nobility as the fundamental economic fact that predetermines other consequences. War, extravagance, and the devaluing of noble land were responsible for the undoing of the nobility in the last phase of the wars and for the general disruption of social relationships. Drouot also argues that the newly-ennobled officials of the administrative and judicial courts blocked the path to social ascension which they themselves had followed. The general consequence is the hardening of class divisions in what was formerly a comparatively fluid social structure.

Georges Livet comments in another fashion on the transfer of property that changed French society as a result of the Wars of Religion. The alienation of church land, together with the confiscation of Protestant goods by Catholics and of *Politique* wealth by the League, is believed to have radically redistributed property. The peasants are thought to have suffered most from the undermining of the old agricultural system. Mass peasant uprisings in the last phases of the wars are seen as a response to both noble brigandage and bourgeois exploitation. Their repercussions were to be felt in the *jacqueries* of subsequent generations. Livet has summarized the recent findings of economic historians who have made particular investigations of the distribution of landed wealth and the effects of the price rise. He concludes that the general position was far more complex and variable than historians such as Hauser and Vaissière have asserted.

The issues presented by the extracts that follow may often appear as differing aspects of the same problems of cause and effect. Yet it is possibly because many of those who have studied the Wars of Religion have been so deeply aware of the diversity of traditions, motives, and beliefs in sixteenth-century France that they have hesitated to offer sweeping generalizations that would order every level of explanation by one determinant dogma. If they have differed in many respects they have generally agreed that the interpretation of the religious wars presents a total problem of vital significance, not only to French, but also to European civilization.

[NOTE: In order to save space, all but a few of the author's footnotes have been eliminated from the original texts of the following readings. Grammar and spelling have been left unchanged.]

CHRONOLOGY

1547		Death of Francis I and accession of Henry II. End of the First Schmalkaldic War of Religion in Germany with the victory of the Emperor Charles V.
1551		Second Assembly of the Council of Trent. Edict of Châteaubriand against heresy.
1552		Alliance of Henry II with the German Protestant Princes. Second Schmalkaldic War. Henry II seizes Metz, Toul, and Verdun. Duke Francis of Guise defends Metz against Charles V.
1555		Peace of Augsburg provides a religious settlement in Germany. Election of Pope Paul IV. Foundation of the Genevan Company of Pastors to evangelize France. The syndicate of the *Grand Parti* at Lyon consolidates the debts of the French monarchy.
1556		Abdication of Charles V in favor of Philip II of Spain. At the invitation of Paul IV, Henry II renews the war with Spain.
1557		The French army under the Constable, Anne de Montmorency, defeated at Saint-Quentin. Bankruptcy of the Spanish monarchy. Protestant riot in Paris in the rue Saint-Jacques.
1558		Guise captures Calais. Protestant demonstrations in Paris at the Pré-aux-Clercs.
1559		Failure of the *Grand Parti* scheme and bankruptcy of the French monarchy.
1559	April	Treaty of Cateau-Cambresis. Death of Paul IV.
	May	Deputies from the Huguenot churches meet in Paris and establish a common French Protestant confession and discipline.
	June	Arrival in Paris of Philip II's envoy, the Duke of Alva, for the marriage by proxy of Elizabeth of Valois, daughter of Henry II and Catherine de Medici, with Philip II. Henry II mortally wounded in a tournament.
	July	Death of Henry II. Accession of Francis II. France governed by Francis of Guise and the Cardinal of Lorraine, uncles of Mary Stuart, the Queen of France.
	August–December	Increased persecution of the Huguenots. Growth of discontent against the Guises. Election of Pope Pius IV.
1560	February	A plot to deprive the Guises of power organised by a group of Huguenot squires led by La Renaudie.
	March	The plot fails at Amboise.
	May	The Edict of Romorantin remits the trial of heretics to ecclesiastical courts. Michel de L'Hôpital appointed Chancellor. He supports the Queen Mother's policy of moderation.
	June	Massacre of Protestants at Lyon.

	July	Death of Mary of Guise, regent of Scotland. Admiral Coligny, the Protestant nephew of the Constable, demands liberty of worship for the Huguenots.
	December	Condé, the Bourbon Protestant leader, sentenced to death for complicity with the conspiracy of Amboise. Death of Francis II. Release of Condé. Meeting of the Estates-General at Orleans. Catherine de Medici secures the regency in the minority of her second son, Charles IX. Anthony of Navarre, elder brother of Condé and First Prince of the Blood, accepts the title of Lieutenant-General and renounces his claim to the regency. His wife, Jeanne d'Albret, publicly professes Calvinism.
1561	January	Catherine de Medici dismisses the Estates-General.
	April	The Catholic leaders, Guise, Montmorency and Marshal Saint-André, form a "triumvirate."
	August	The Estates-General meet at Pontoise in anti-clerical mood. Demands for the confiscation of Church property.
	September	The French Catholic Church undertakes partial responsibility for the monarchy's debts by the Contract of Poissy. Catherine de Medici arranges a meeting of Catholic and Calvinist clergy at Poissy, but hopes of compromise are disappointed. Clash between the Cardinal of Lorraine and Calvin's lieutenant, Théodore de Bèze. The Jesuit leader, Lainez, denounces the intentions of the regency. Sympathies for Calvinism revealed at court and within a section of the episcopacy.
	October–December	Religious riots in Paris and other large towns. Military organization of the Huguenot churches completed.
1562	January	Edict of Saint-Germain grants toleration to the Huguenots. Opening of the third assembly of the Council of Trent.
	March	Massacre of Huguenots at Vassy by the Duke of Guise. The Queen Mother appeals to Condé, but is escorted to Paris with Charles IX by the triumvirate. Anthony of Navarre associated with the Catholic party.
	April–May	Condé establishes his base at Orleans. Massacres and religious riots occur throughout the principal towns. Cruelties of the Huguenot commander, Des Adrets, in Dauphiné and of the Catholic, Blaise de Montluc, in Gascony.
	July	Negotiations for peace fail. General hostilities begin.
	August	Campaign of Guise and Saint-André on the Loire. Spanish and Papal troops reinforce the Catholic armies. Mercenaries are hired in the Swiss cantons by the triumvirate and in Germany by D'Andelot, Coligny's brother.
	September	Alliance between Elizabeth of England and Condé. English occupation of Le Havre.
	October	Capture of Rouen by the Catholics.
	November	Death of Anthony of Navarre.
	December	Battle of Dreux. Death of Saint-André. Capture of Montmorency by the Huguenots and of Condé by the Catholic forces.
1563	February	Assassination of Guise during his siege of Orléans. Coligny condones the act.

	March	Peace of Amboise, granting degrees of toleration to Protestants according to social status.
	August	Fourth Huguenot synod at Lyon purges the movement of congregationalist influences.
1564	March	The court begins an eighteen-month tour of the provinces.
	April	Peace of Troyes with England.
	May	Death of Calvin.
1565	January	Clash in Paris between the Cardinal of Lorraine and Marshal Francis of Montmorency, eldest son of the Constable.
	June	Catherine de Medici and Charles IX meet Elisabeth of Valois and Alva at Bayonne.
1566		L'Hôpital's legal and administrative reforms issued at Moulins. Pius V elected to the Papacy. Religious riots and armed resistance to Philip II in the Netherlands.
1567	July–August	Alva marches through Franche-Comté, Lorraine, and Luxemburg on his way to suppress the Netherlands. The French monarchy distrusts the purpose of Alva's march and hires Swiss mercenaries. The Huguenots assume collusion between Alva and the monarchy.
	September	Huguenot conspiracy to seize the court at Meaux. Second civil war begins.
	October	Massacre of Catholics at Nîmes.
	November	Indecisive battle of Saint-Denis. Death of Constable Montmorency.
1568	March	Edict of Longjumeau restores the peace of Amboise.
	July	Alva defeats Louis of Nassau, brother of William of Orange, at Jemmingen.
	August	Failure of an attempt by the monarchy to arrest Condé and Coligny. The Huguenot leaders retire to La Rochelle. Third civil war begins.
	October	Expedition of William of Orange in the Netherlands, supported by Huguenots and German mercenaries.
	December	Orange withdraws to France.
1569	March	The Duke of Anjou, Catherine's third son, defeats the Huguenot army at Jarnac. Death of Condé. Coligny as Huguenot leader.
	May	Wolfgang von Zweibrücken leads a German army to support Coligny.
	August	Coligny abandons the siege of Poitiers defended by Henry of Guise, son and successor of the Duke.
	October	Anjou defeats Coligny. Anjou checked at Saint-Jean d'Angély. Coligny marches to the Rhône.
1570	June	Coligny, attempting to join a new German army led by William of Orange, fights an indecisive engagement with Marshal de Cossé at Arnay-le-Duc.
	August	Peace of Saint-Germain, granting the Huguenots La Rochelle, Montauban, Cognac and La Charité as security towns.
1571	February	Massacre of Protestants at Orange.
	September	Coligny arrives at the French court.

	OCTOBER	Spanish victory of Lepanto against the Turks. Exposure of the Ridolfi plot against Elizabeth of England on behalf of Mary Queen of Scots.
1572	MARCH	Negotiations between Catherine de Medici and Jeanne d'Albret for the marriage of their respective children, Marguerite of Valois and Henry of Navarre. Elizabeth of England expels the rebel Netherlands fleet under La Marck.
	APRIL	La Marck seizes Brille. General revolt in the northern Netherlands. Alliance between France and England.
	MAY	Death of Pius V. Election of Gregory XIII. Mons taken by Louis of Nassau with the support of Genlis' Huguenot contingent.
	JUNE	Resistance of Catherine de Medici to the policy of war with Spain. Doubts about the support of Elizabeth of England. Coligny enters Paris. Death of Jeanne d'Albret. Coligny opposed in the Council on the question of war in Flanders.
	JULY	Defeat of Genlis by Alva. Alva protests to Catherine de Medici.
	AUGUST 4	Return of Catherine de Medici to Paris. Her endeavours to prevent war with Spain.
	AUGUST 10	Coligny outvoted in the Council on the Spanish War. Massacre of Huguenots at Troyes.
	AUGUST 18	Marriage of Marguerite of Valois and Henry of Navarre.
	AUGUST 22	An attempt to assassinate Coligny fails. Charles IX promises satisfaction to the Huguenots.
	AUGUST 23	Charles IX persuaded to sanction the killing of the Huguenot leaders.
	AUGUST 24	Massacre of St. Bartholomew. Henry of Navarre and Henry of Condé (son of Louis of Condé) abjure Protestantism. Fourth civil war.
	SEPTEMBER	Fall of Mons.
1573	JANUARY–APRIL	Siege of La Rochelle. Formation of a malcontent group round Catherine de Medici's fourth son, the Duke of Alençon, and the Montmorency family. This group provides the basis of the *politique* faction, favouring toleration.
	MAY	Anjou elected King of Poland.
	JUNE	Treaty of La Rochelle.
	AUGUST	Formation of Huguenot federative republics in Languedoc and Upper Guienne.
1574	FEBRUARY	*Politique* conspiracy of Navarre, Alençon, and Marshals Montmorency and Cossé. Escape of Condé from court. His appeal to the German princes. Fifth civil war begins.
	MARCH	Death of Charles IX.
	AUGUST	A federal constitution drawn up by Huguenot deputies at Millau.
	SEPTEMBER	Return of Anjou to France as Henry III. Alliance of Damville (the Constable Montmorency's second son) in Languedoc with the Huguenots.
	DECEMBER	Death of the Cardinal of Lorraine.
1575	FEBRUARY	Articles of Union between Huguenots and *Politiques* drawn up at Nîmes.
	SEPTEMBER	Escape and revolt of Alençon. Invasion of John Casimir of the Palatinate in support of the Huguenots.

1576	FEBRUARY	Escape of Navarre from Court.
	MARCH	Junction of Alençon and Casimir.
	MAY	Peace of Monsieur. Extension of those conditions of toleration allowed at the Peace of Saint-Germain. Alençon becomes Duke of Anjou. Government of Picardy given to Condé.
	JUNE	Catholic League formed in Picardy under the leadership of the Guises to oppose the peace. Henry III attempts to prevent the spread of the League, and then declares his support for it.
	DECEMBER	Meeting of the Estates General at Blois without Protestant representation. Demand for renewal of war by the Estates-General hindered by their refusal to vote supplies. Representatives of the Estates admitted to the Council to supervise the royal administration.
1577	MARCH	Dissolution of the Estates-General. Sixth civil war. Anjou deserts the Huguenots.
	MAY	Damville makes a separate peace with Henry III. Capture of La Charité by Catholic forces.
	SEPTEMBER	Peace of Bergerac. The monarchy reforms the monetary system. Abolition of the *livre tournois* as the basic standard of value.
1578	JANUARY	Defeat of William of Orange at Gemblours.
	FEBRUARY–APRIL	Affrays at the French Court between the swordsmen of the King, Anjou and Guise.
	JULY	Anjou at Mons as defender of the liberties of the Netherlands.
	OCTOBER	Death of Philip II's half-brother, Don John of Austria. Alessandro Farnese, Duke of Parma, appointed Governor of the Netherlands in his place. Casimir of the Palatinate leads a German-English force to support William of Orange.
1579	JANUARY	Union of Arras among the southern Catholic provinces of the Netherlands. The northern provinces respond with the Union of Utrecht.
	FEBRUARY	Catherine de Medici journeys in Guienne and Languedoc and negotiates a pacification for the area. Ordinance of Blois reforms the royal administration.
	MAY	The Union of Arras comes to terms with Parma.
	NOVEMBER	Condé seizes La Fère on the Netherlands frontier.
	DECEMBER	The Assembly of the Clergy at Melun denounces the sale of ecclesiastical property by the monarchy.
1580	JANUARY	Seventh civil war begins in southern France.
	FEBRUARY	Discussions at Nancy between Casimir, Mayenne (Guise's brother), and Duke Charles of Lorraine to concert action against Henry III.
	MAY	Navarre takes Cahors. Rivalry of Condé and Navarre for the leadership of the Huguenot movement.
	SEPTEMBER	Anjou accepts the sovereignty of the Netherlands.
	NOVEMBER	Peace of Fleix ends the war in the south.
1581		Anjou betrothed to Elizabeth of England.
1582		French expedition to the Azores to aid the Portuguese pretender against Philip II.

1583	JANUARY	Anjou fails in an attempt to seize Antwerp.
	JUNE	The French defeated in the Azores. Anjou withdraws from the Netherlands.
1584	MAY	The Duke of Epernon, Henry III's most powerful favourite, visits Henry of Navarre to urge him to accept Catholicism.
	JUNE	Death of Anjou.
	JULY	Assassination of William of Orange. Henry of Navarre heir presumptive to Henry III. Renewal of the Catholic League, opposing the succession of Henry of Navarre. Organisation of the Sixteen in Paris represents the popular element in the League.
1585	JANUARY	Treaty of Joinville between Spain and the Guises.
	JULY	Henry III submits to the League by the Treaty of Nemours.
	AUGUST	Parma captures Antwerp.
	SEPTEMBER	The newly elected Pope Sixtus V excommunicates Navarre and Condé.
	DECEMBER	Leicester's English army lands in the Netherlands.
1586		Negotiations between Catherine de Medici and Henry of Navarre. The League obliges Henry III to declare war against the Huguenots.
1587	MARCH	Execution of Mary Queen of Scots.
	AUGUST	A large mercenary German army, recruited by Navarre and Casimir enters Lorraine.
	OCTOBER	Navarre defeats the royal army under Joyeuse at Coutras.
	NOVEMBER	Guise defeats the Germans at Auneau. Epernon prevents the destruction of the German army, and escorts it to the frontier.
1588	FEBRUARY	Eleven Articles, prepared at Nancy by the Guises to restrict the King's authority, presented at court.
	MARCH	Death of Henry of Condé. Mendoza, the Spanish ambassador, conspires with the League to neutralise the King and provide shelter for the Armada in the ports of Picardy.
	APRIL	Epernon forced by the League to retire to Normandy.
	MAY 9	Guise enters Paris in defiance of Henry III.
	MAY 12	The King's guards and Swiss troops enter Paris. Barricades raised in the streets by the crowds supporting Guise. The King escapes from his capital.
	MAY 17–20	A revolutionary commune established in Paris.
	JULY	The King again capitulates to the League by the Edict of Union.
	AUGUST	The defeat of the Armada.
	SEPTEMBER	The King dismisses the secretaries of State appointed by Catherine de Medici.
	OCTOBER	The Estates-General, dominated by the League, meet at Blois. The Duke of Savoy invades Saluzzo.
	DECEMBER	Guise and his brother, the Cardinal of Guise, assassinated by order of Henry III. Certain members of the League in the Estates-General arrested.
1589	JANUARY	Open revolt of the League in Paris and elsewhere. Mayenne as the leader of the League. Death of Catherine de Medici.

	February	Mayenne declared Lieutenant-General by the League's Council of Forty.
	April	Alliance of Henry III and Henry of Navarre. Split within the League between aristocratic and popular pro-Spanish elements.
	May	Sixtus V excommunicates Henry III and absolves his subjects from their allegiance.
	July	Assassination of Henry III. Henry of Navarre's uncle, the Cardinal of Bourbon, declared King by the League as Charles X, but remains in captivity.
	September	Henry IV (Henry of Navarre) defeats Mayenne at Arques.
1590	January	The League in Provence divided between the factions of the Count of Carcès and the Countess of Saulx.
	March	Henry IV defeats Mayenne at Ivry.
	May	Henry IV besieges Paris. Death of Charles X. Peasant revolt of the *gauthiers* in Normandy.
	September	Parma and the Spanish army of the Netherlands relieve Paris.
	November	The Duke of Savoy enters Aix-en-Provence.
1591	February	The regime of Charles de Casaulx established in Marseille.
	May	Spanish and English armies enter the conflict in Brittany.
	July	Declaration of Mantes by Henry IV acknowledging Catholicism as the religion of state.
	August	The son of Henry of Guise acclaimed in Paris.
	October	Death of Pope Gregory XIV.
	November	The Sixteen terrorize Paris. They purge the *Parlement* and are suppressed by Mayenne.
1592	March	Parma relieves Rouen but dies (December) as a result of a wound received in the campaign. Destruction of peasant armies in Brittany.
1593	January	The Estates-General convoked by Mayenne at Paris to choose a successor to Charles X. Growing anti-Spanish feeling amid the upper classes of the League.
	May	Feria, the Spanish ambassador, proposes the Infanta as Queen of France.
	June	The *Parlement* of Paris upholds the Salic Law, forbidding the transmission of the crown by the female line. Brigandage and peasant revolt in Brittany.
	July	Henry IV abjures Protestantism.
1594	January	Epernon establishes himself as Governor of Provence and defies Henry IV. He negotiates with Damville, the ruler of Languedoc.
	March	Henry IV secures Paris and Rouen. The rising of the desperate peasant *croquants* of Périgord and Limousin.
	November	The son of Henry of Guise comes to terms with Henry IV and is appointed Governor of Provence.
	December	Charles of Lorraine makes peace with Henry IV.
1595	January	Henry IV declares war against Spain.

	FEBRUARY	Huguenot deputies at Saumur reveal the hostility of the movement to the King since his conversion. Withdrawal of the English contingents supporting Henry IV. Continued resistance of Mercoeur in Brittany and Mayenne in Burgundy.
	JUNE	Henry IV wins a reckless engagement at Fontaine-Française against the Spanish.
	AUGUST	Death of the Duke of Nemours, the Leaguer leader in Lyonnais.
	SEPTEMBER	Absolution granted Henry IV by Pope Clement VIII.
	DECEMBER	Defeat of Epernon by Guise and Lesdiguières, the ruler of Dauphiné. Submission of Mayenne by the Edict of Folembray.
1596	FEBRUARY	Overthrow of Casaulx in Marseille.
	APRIL	The Spanish take Calais.
	MAY	Henry IV evicts the Spanish garrison from La Fère, despite desertion by the Huguenot contingents.
1597	MARCH	The Spanish secure Amiens.
	SEPTEMBER	Amiens regained by Henry IV.
1598	MARCH	Submission of Mercoeur.
	APRIL	The Edict of Nantes grants toleration to the Huguenots.
	MAY	The Peace of Vervins ends the war with Spain.
	SEPTEMBER	Death of Philip II.

The Conflict of Opinion

"The weight of evidence is increasingly in favor of the view that the causes of the Huguenot movement were as much if not more political and economic than religious."

— James Westfall Thompson

"If the self-interested defenders of the Roman Church — the Guises, supported by the mighty King of Spain — had not sworn to exterminate Protestantism, our country would have been spared this war and all its sorrowful consequences."

— Samuel Mours

"While these shreds of evidence are not conclusive, and while there is nothing to tie these inciting activities directly to Geneva, it is clear that in some areas, Calvin's envoys were responsible for stimulating war fervor and even rioting on behalf of the common cause. . . . By no means pacifist, he [Calvin] accepted and supported religious war in exceedingly realistic ways."

— Robert Kingdon

"It cannot be denied that selfish passion and sometimes unrestrained greed persuaded many of the nobility and captains to join the Protestants. Study of the social background would reveal that the ruined heirs of feudal families merely awaited a chance to find a breach in the fortress of the royal power and to reconstitute their fortunes by any means they found at hand. The wealth of the Church . . . seemed a standing offense to this impoverished class.

— Lucien Romier

"We have in the course of this narrative noted blunder after blunder in Catherine's policy, and these, coupled with her shortcomings of character and intellect, undoubtedly affected the nature and duration of France's hirty-odd years of disaster."

— Sir John Neale

"There is a limit to a policy of compassion and to respect for the ideas and lives of individuals — the public good. Catherine de Medici had too good a head on her shoulders to forget it."

— Jean Héritier

"The absurd conclusion that Paris and St. Bartholomew preserved the national unity, that Charles IX and the Guises performed the role of the Convention of 1793, . . . is a bizarre and eccentric paradox, displaying impartiality without sympathy, making a friend of our enemy, and utterly lacking in compassion for the slaughtered precursors of liberty."

— Jules Michelet

"The associations of artisans dominated the League and formed that alliance which always results from the link between the clergy and the lower classes in Catholic countries — an alliance between the material force of labour and the persuasive influence of the Holy Gospel. The League had the effect of imprinting a stronger spirit of liberty upon the commune, and of awakening within it that ferment of popular independence which we have seen breaking forth in Paris in the barricades of 1588, in the organisation of the Sixteen, and in the sovereign alliance of cities with cities."

— J.-B.-H. Capefigue

"If one wished to describe the character of the struggle of Paris against King Henry III and to define the spirit of the League, one would say that it was a . . . movement inspired by the Holy See, Spain, and the clergy, led by the Guises and using as its instrument the least enlightened part of the people of Paris."

— Paul Robiquet

"The League was not just an alliance of fervent Catholics, nor was it merely an instrument at the disposal of the Guises. It was a rolling back of the processes of time, a return to the advantages of past conditions which the monarchy had opposed and then partially suppressed. In particular it was a return to the independent urban life of the city states."

— Fernand Braudel

"New social antagonisms arose and existing antipathies deepened. Religion might dress up these antagonisms in its own colours or strengthen them with fanaticism, but it was these class hatreds that served as the basis of local conflicts at the time of the League. The general crisis of the nobility during the religious wars is a recognised fact, but it is not always recognised that it is a fundamental fact from which many consequences follow."

— Henri Drouot

"The Wars of Religion exacerbated or burst the abscesses of social discontent, but it is the ruin of the old agricultural system, accompanied by the expropriation of the peasantry, that explains in part the popular disturbances of the seventeenth century."

— Georges Livet

I. CAUSES

The Domination of Political Motives

JAMES WESTFALL THOMPSON

The interests of James Westfall Thompson (1869–1941) were directed more toward medieval Germany than to Renaissance France. His study of feudal Germany and his general economic and social history of Europe in the middle ages may be the works by which he is best remembered, but his book on the early phases of the French Wars of Religion, from which the following extract has been taken, has for long been the only detailed general account of political and military events available in English. Thompson held the Chair of Medieval History at the University of Chicago for many years until his appointment as Professor of European History to the University of California in 1932. He retired as Professor Emeritus in 1939.

IT IS to be observed that the Huguenots were concerted not only for religious, but for political interests. The distinction was fully appreciated at the time, the former being called "Huguenots of religion" and the latter "Huguenots of state." The former were Calvinists who were resolved no longer to endure the cruelties of religious oppression; the latter — mostly nobles — those opposed to the monopoly of power enjoyed by the Guises. The weight of evidence is increasingly in favour of the view that the causes of the Huguenot movement were as much if not more political and economic than religious.

It was only in the general dislocation and *désœuvrement* of society that followed the cessation of the foreign wars that the French began to realize the weight of the burdens which their governmental system laid upon them. . . . Until . . . the religious sense gave a voice to the dumb discontent, social or political, first in the Huguenot rising and afterward in the outbreak of the League, there was little to show the real force of the opposition to the established order.

Abstractly considered, the religious Huguenots were not very dangerous to the state so long as they confined their activity to the discussion of doctrine. This could not easily be done, however, nor did the opponents of the church so desire; for the church was a social and political fabric, as well as a spiritual institution, and to challenge or deny its spiritual sovereignty meant also to invalidate its social and political claims, so that the whole structure was compromised. Thus the issue of religion raised by the Huguenots merged imperceptibly into that of the political Huguenots, who not only wanted to alter the foundations of belief, but to change the institutional order of things, and who used the religious opposition as a means to attack the authority of the crown. The most active of this class were the nobles, possessed of lands or bred to the profession of arms, whom a species of political atavism actuated to endeavour to

From James Westfall Thompson, *The Wars of Religion in France,* second edition (New York, n.d.), pp. 16–20, 26–28, 65–68, 140–142. Reprinted by permission of Frederick Ungar Publishing Company.

recover that feudal power which the noblesse had enjoyed before the powerful kings like Louis IX and Philip IV coerced the baronage; before the Hundred-Years' War ruined them; before Louis XI throttled the League of the Public Weal in 1465. The weakness of Francis II, the minority of the crown under Charles IX, and above all, the dissatisfaction of princes of the blood and the old aristocracy, like the Montmorencys, with the upstart pretensions and power of the Guises — these causes united to make the Huguenots of state a formidable political party. Religion and politics together provoked the long series of civil wars whose termination was not until Henry IV brought peace and prosperity to France again in 1598.

It is necessary to picture the state of France at this time. The French were not essentially an industrial or commercial nation in the sixteenth century. France had almost no maritime power and its external commerce was not great. The great majority of the French people was composed of peasants, small proprietors, artisans and officials. If we analyse city society, we find first some artisans and small merchants — the bourgeois and the *gens-de-robe* forming the upper class. The towns had long since ceased to govern themselves. Society was aristocratic and controlled by the clergy and nobility. The upper clergy was very rich. High prelates were all grand seigneurs, while the lower clergy was very dependent. Monks abounded in the towns, and the curates possessed a certain influence. The most powerful class was the nobles, seigneurs, and gentlemen, who possessed a great portion of the rural properties, and still had fortified castles. They were wholly employed either at court or in war, or held appointments as governors of provinces and captains of strongholds. The nobles alone constituted the regular companies of cavalry, that is to say, the dominant element of the army. This class was therefore of influence in the state and the most material force in society.

The government was an absolute monarchy. The king was theoretically uncontested master and obeyed by all; he exercised an arbitrary and uncontrolled power, and could decide according to his pleasure, with reference to taxes, laws, and affairs both of state and of the church, save in matters of faith. He named and revoked the commissions of all the governors and acted under the advice of a council composed of the princes of the blood and favorites. But this absolute authority was still personal. The king was only obeyed upon condition of giving the orders himself. There was no conception of an abstract kingship. If the king abandoned the power to a favorite, the other great personages of the court would refuse to obey, and declare that the sovereign was a prisoner. Everything depended upon a single person. No one thought of resisting Francis I or Henry II because they were men grown at their accession. But after 1559 we find a series of royal infants or an indolent monarch like Henry III. Then began the famous rivalries between the great nobles, rivalries out of which were born the political parties of the times, in which the Guises, the Montmorencys and the famous Châtillon brothers figure so prominently.

Fundamentally speaking, the aims of both classes of Huguenots were revolutionary, and were directed, the one against the authority of the medieval church, the other against the authority of the French monarchy. The latter was a feudal manifestation, not yet republican. The republican nature of early political Huguenotism has been exaggerated. There was no such feeling at all as early as 1560, and even at the height of Huguenot activity and power in 1570–72, most men still felt that the state of France was *vrayement monarchique,* and that the structure of society and the genius of the people was strongly inclined to the form of government which eight centuries of development had evolved; that it was searching for false liberty by perilous methods to seek fundamentally to alter the state. In a word, most political Huguenots in 1560 were reformers, not revolutionists; the extremists were Calvinist zealots and those of selfish purposes who were working for their own ends. For in every great movement there are always those who seek to exploit the cause. Mixed with both classes of Huguenots were those who sought to fish in troubled waters, who, under the guise of religion or the public good, took occasion to pillage and rob all persons, of whatever degree or quality; who plundered cities, pulled down churches, carried off relics, burnt towns, destroyed castles, seized the revenues of the church and the king, informed for the sake of reward, and enriched themselves by the confiscated property of others. Similar things are not less true of the Catholics. For there were zealots and fanatics among them also, who under pretext of religion and patriotism were guilty of great iniquity and heaped up much ill-gotten wealth.

The ascendency of the Guises quite as much as the suppressive measures of the government against Calvinism served to bring this disaffection to a head. The issues, either way, cannot be separated. The practical aims of the Guises were large enough to create dismay without it being necessary to believe that as early as 1560 they aimed to secure the crown by deposing the house of Valois. It was unreasonable to suppose, though it proved to be so in the end, that the four sons of Henry II would all die heirless, and even in the event of that possibility, the house of Bourbon still remained to sustain the principle of primogeniture.

. . . The spirit of unrest in France, both political and religious, was so great that only a head was wanting, not members, in order to bring things to a focus. The whole of Aquitaine and Normandy was reported, in December 1559, to be in such "good heart" as to be easily excited to action if they perceived any movement elsewhere; in February 1560, the turbulence in Paris was so great that Coligny was appointed to go thither in advance of the King's entrance "for the appeasing of the garboil there." In order to repress this spirit of rebellion the government diligently prosecuted the Huguenots. The Guises hoped that the severity exercised during the last few months in Paris and many other cities against persons condemned for their religion, of whom very great numbers were burnt alive, would terrify Calvinists and the political Huguenots into obedience. But, on the contrary, local rebellion increased. At Rouen, at Bordeaux, and between Blois and Orleans, Huguenots arrested by the King's officers were rescued by armed bands, in some cases the officers being killed. Indeed, so common did these practices become that they were at last heard of without surprise.

> Imagine a young king [wrote the Venetian ambassador] without experience and without authority; a council rent by discord; the royal authority in the hands of a woman alternately wise, timid, and irresolute, and always a woman; the people divided into factions and the prey of insolent agitators who under pretense of religious zeal trouble the public repose, corrupt manners, disparage the law, check the administration of justice, and imperil the royal authority.

The interests of the religious Huguenots and the political Huguenots continued to approach during the autumn and winter of 1559–60. In order to make head against the usurpation of the Guises, which they represented as a foreign domination, the latter contended that it was necessary to call the estates of France in order to interpret the laws, just as the Calvinists contended for an interpretation of the Scriptures. The contentions of the Huguenots, the tyrannical conduct of the Guises, the menaces which they did not hesitate to utter against the high nobles of the realm, the retirement into which they had driven the constable, the removal of the princes of the blood which they had brought about upon one pretext or another, the contempt they expressed for the States-General, the corruption of justice, their exorbitant financial policy, the disposal of offices and benefices which they practiced — all these causes, united with religious persecutions, constituted a body of grievances for which redress inevitably would be demanded. The question was, How? The leaders of the Huguenots — and the term is used even more in a political sense than in a religious one— were not ignorant of the history of the Reformation in Germany, nor unaware of the fact that politics had been commingled with religion there.

. . . The demand for the States-General [in the later months of 1560] was the voice of France, speaking through the noblesse and the bourgeoisie, crying out for a thorough inquiry into the administration of the Guises and reformation of the governmental system of both state and church; as such it was a menace to the cardinal and his brother and in alignment with the demands of the political Huguenots. The costly wars of Henry II, the extravagance of the court; the burdensome taxation; the venality of justice; the lawlessness and disorder prevailing everywhere; the impoverishment of many noble families, and the rise of new nobles out of the violence of the wars in Picardy and Italy, more prone to license and less softened by the social graces that characterized the old families; the dilapidation of ancestral fortunes and the displacements of wealth; the religious unrest; the corruption of the church — all these grievances, none of which was wholly new, were piling up with a cumulative force, whose impending attack the Guises regarded with great apprehension.

The administration of the cardinal of Lorraine and his ducal brother had not mended matters, but in justice to them it should be said that their ministry was quite as much the occasion as the cause of the popular outcry for reform. The evils of the former reign were reaching a climax which their haughtiness and ambition served to accentuate. Misappropriation of public moneys, exorbitant taxation, denial of justice, spoliation of the crown lands, especially the forests, the dilapidation of church property, and the corruption of manners, were undoubtedly the deepest popular grievances. In the demand for redress of these grievances all honest men were united. In 1560 the cry of the Huguenots for freedom of worship was the voice of a minority of them only. Most Huguenots at this time were political and not religious Huguenots, who simply used the demand of the new religionists as a vehicle of expression; this sentiment also accounts for local risings to rescue arrested Calvinists, the participants in many cases being actuated more by the desire to make a demonstration against the government than by sympathy with the Calvinist doctrines.

The debts of the crown at the accession of Francis II aggregated forty-three millions of livres, upon which interest had to be paid, without including pensions and salaries due to officers and servants of the royal household, and the gendarmerie, which were from two to five years in arrears, a sum so great that if the entire revenue of the crown for a decade could have been devoted to its discharge, it would not have been possible to liquidate it. The result was the provinces abounded with poor men driven to live by violence and crime, while even the nobility, because of their reduced incomes, and the soldiery on account of arrears of wages, were driven to plunder the people. Even members of the judiciary and the clergy had recourse to illicit practices. The regular provincial administration was powerless to suppress evils so prevalent, whose roots were found in the condition of society. It was in vain that the crown announced that it was illegal to have recourse to arms for redress of injuries and commanded the governors in the provinces, the bailiffs, seneschals, and other similar officers to stay within their jurisdictions and vigilantly to sustain the provost-marshals in suppressing sedition or illegal assemblies. Some men thought the remedy lay in more drastic penalties and advocated the abolishment of appeal in criminal causes, as in Italy and Flanders. But history, in many epochs shows that the social maladies of a complex society cannot be so cured.

* * *

Although the purposes of the Huguenots were clandestinely more political than religious, it was expedient to cloak them under a mantle of faith. The political organization of the Huguenots was effected through the medium of an association, a form of organization of which there are many examples, both Protestant and Catholic, during this troubled period. The preamble of the instrument of government disclaimed any private motives or considerations on the part of those who were parties to the association, and asserted that their sole purpose was to liberate the King from "captivity" and punish the insolence and tyranny of the disloyal and the enemies of the church. Idolatry, blasphemy, violence, and robbery were forbidden within the territory of the association, in order that all might know that it had "the fear of God before it." The association was to expire after the King had attained his majority.

The essential difficulties in the situation as it obtained at this time are manifest. The Huguenots declared the King to be a captive in the hands of the Guises and themselves claimed to be loyal subjects in rebellion against tyranny. The Guises, on the other hand, branded the Huguenots as rebels and schismatics, although Catherine de Medici still had a lingering hope of restoring peace, and in official utterances carefully refrained from alluding to the prince of Condé as a rebel. Neither side would agree to lay down its arms without the other doing likewise, and neither dared take the initiative in this matter. The situation, therefore, was an irreconcilable one, which nothing but war could settle. The political determinations of the Huguenots were quite as fixed as their religious convictions, for part of their platform was the article agreed upon by the estates at Orleans to the effect that the cardinal of Lorraine, the duke of Guise, the constable, and the marshals Brissac and St. André, should render an account of their stewardship. How far politics governed the situation is evidenced by the fact that late in April the king of Navarre and Montmorency began to weaken in their attitude when it was known that Condé dominated the middle Loire country, Touraine, Maine, Anjou, and much of Normandy; when it was learned that the cities of Lyons, Toulouse, Caen, Rouen, Dieppe, Troyes, Bourges, and the provinces of Dauphiné, Provence, and Poitou, had declared for the Huguenot cause; and when troops were pouring into Orleans by thousands.

Calvinist Religious Aggression

ROBERT M. KINGDON

Professor Kingdon was born in 1927 and pursued his university studies at Oberlin College, Columbia University and the University of Geneva. Much of his research has been conducted in the Genevan archives. Apart from his study of the role of Geneva in the coming of the religious wars in France (from which the ensuing passages have been taken), he has prepared, with M. Jean-François Bergier, an edition of the registers of the Genevan Company of Pastors in the years 1546–1564 (Geneva, 2 vols., 1962–64). He has also recently published an edition of two sixteenth-century pamphlets by William Cecil and William Allen concerning the status of English Catholics under the Elizabethan religious settlement, a task entrusted to him by his late teacher, Garret Mattingly. Dr. Kingdon has held a number of teaching posts in American universities and is now Professor of History at the University of Wisconsin and secretary of the American Society for Reformation Research.

Calvin and the members of the Company of Pastors at first devoted most of their time to consolidating the Reformation in Geneva, for they still faced local opposition from some factions. They gradually gained ground, with the support of the hundreds of French religious refugees who increasingly sought asylum there. Opposition came to a climax early in 1555, when several prominent local citizens, among them one Ami Perrin, incited and led a riot that was intended to expel all the French from the city. The riot was promptly suppressed: Perrin and his friends fled; their accomplices were executed. Thus Calvin's power was finally consolidated locally, and he was at last free to devote all his time and energy to the larger task of evangelizing his native France.

. . . By 1557 the sending of emissaries to France had become a regular part of the Geneva Company's business. In that year eleven churches received pastors; in 1558, twenty-two, in 1559 thirty-two; and in 1560, 1561 and 1562 twelve churches each year. (These figures taken from the official Register of the Company do not reveal that 1561 was actually the peak year, when, as we learn from records supplementing the Register, more than one hundred men were sent out.) In 1562 just subsequent to the most substantial dispatch of pastors, the religious ferment to which these men had ministered finally roused passions to an intensity that flared into the war that would continue, with only minor pauses, for forty years. Only seven years had elapsed between the inception of the Geneva Company's concentrated missionary effort and the beginning of the French religious wars.

. . . Though we have only slight evidence on the way in which books were sent into France, there is ample evidence that they did indeed arrive and deeply affect the thinking and action of millions of Frenchmen. Any Catholic chronicler is willing enough to testify to that. Claude Haton, for example, writing on the political events of Paris late in 1561 noted that from Geneva were arriving a great quantity of theological works and "a great other number of little booklets, like the Marotic and

From Robert M. Kingdon, *Geneva and the Coming of the Wars of Religion in France* (Geneva, 1956), pp. 1, 2, 103, 106, 108–112. Reprinted by permission of the author and Librairie E. Droz, Geneva.

Bezian Psalms . . . and other booklets titled *Catechism of the true religion,* the *Buckler of the faith,* the *Bastion of the faith,* and infinite other books . . . all well bound in red and black calf, some well gilded," for sale at the Court and in Paris. A chronicler more sympathetic to the Protestants notes that the Cardinal of Lorraine was able to collect, in 1560, just after the collapse of the Conspiracy of Amboise, which had been aimed partially at him, some twenty-two pamphlets attacking him personally.

Propaganda from Geneva was unquestionably being widely disseminated in France, particularly in 1561 and 1562 when royal refusal to enforce all the anti-Protestant edicts encouraged open sale of the literature produced in Geneva. Unquestionably, too, the results of the wide distribution were most disturbing to ecclesiastical and political authorities, for the flood of books must have been a most substantial support to the men from Geneva in their efforts to reform religion radically in France. These books must be given partial credit for the revolutionary temper that helped produce war in 1562.

. . . The Calvinist tide of men and propaganda reached its crest in 1562. Now it could no longer be contained by the dikes of traditional French society. This was especially so since the French monarchy early in 1562 slipped away from Huguenot influence, back to the influence of the fanatically Catholic Guises. The Duke of Guise, after covering himself against German attack by persuading the Duke of Württemberg that he was much interested in the Lutheran, as opposed to the Calvinist brand of Protestantism, marched home and, early in March 1562, slaughtered a congregation of Calvinists holding church services in the small town of Vassy in his own domains, then went on in triumph to Catholic Paris to rejoin the Court and bring it once again under his dominance. Within a few weeks, his actions had provoked war.

. . . A high percentage, perhaps even the majority, of the French nobility, supported Condé's cause; nobles were an outstanding element in the newly organised army, and others organised local armies in various provinces. Hubert Languet, the noted humanist and legist, who was in Paris at this time as the Elector of Saxony's Ambassador to the French, in mid-April reported that the leaders of the Huguenot armies were the Prince de Rohan, Condé, the Lord de Grammont for the Navarre area, and the Lord de "Monbrun" for the Dauphiné-Languedoc area, and that Coligny also held an important position. All of the men Languet mentions were hard-core Protestants, who steadfastly maintained the Calvinist quarrel.

Signatures on Condé's Orleans manifesto identify other noble leaders of the revolting army:

> De Condé, de Jean de Rohan, de Larochefoucauld, de Coligny, du prince de Portein, de d'Andelot, de Piennes, de Soubize, d'Ivoy, de Morvilliers, de Genlis, de Canny, etc etc "and four thousand gentlemen of the best and most ancient houses of France, who accompany monseigneur the prince"

These leaders of the French nobility were soon joined in Orleans by leaders of the French Protestant ministry, most prominent among them Beza. The National Synod held in Orleans only a few weeks later, brought to Beza's side delegates from all the churches in France. Conrad Badius, the erstwhile Geneva printer turned pastor, and Jean Ribittus, and François Berauld, both professors at the University of Geneva, arrived in Orleans before the issuance of the declaration of Condé to help in strengthening the Huguenot cause.

These ecclesiastical leaders constituted a war party around Condé. They were opposed to any negotiations or military maneuvres that, in the interest of strategy or a peaceful settlement, would sacrifice Protestant congregations or their legal right to worship. Beza, as noted, had opposed the abandonment of Paris in March, and he later proposed an armed seizure of Paris. He did what he could to prevent Condé from honoring an offer to leave the kingdom, which Catherine de Medici had tricked him into making. Beza seems constantly to have tried to make Condé stand firm and fight.

I have shown, briefly, the alacrity with which the Protestant leaders, both lay and clerical, responded to the call for war. For a concrete picture of the mobilization of the Huguenot soldiery, the actual backbone of the army, let us turn to documentation of mustering and mobilization in the provinces. To begin with, there were remnants of the military organisation La Renaudie had prepared for the Conspiracy of Amboise. In Provence, for example, Paul de Mouvans had organised a small army in 1560 to assist the Conspiracy; after the slaughter at Amboise he disbanded this troop and fled to Geneva. Early in 1562 he came back to Provence, organised the remnants of his company, and began his guerrilla war again. Religious war began a good three months earlier in Provence than in the rest of France.

For the mobilization in Guyenne there is even better documentation. In November, 1560, the Guyenne Synod of Clairac, presided over by Pastor Boisnormand, the ministerial conspirator of Amboise, ordered the churches of the province to begin organising military cadres. In November 1561, this work was completed by the Synod of Upper Guyenne meeting at Sainte-Foy. The gentlemen present elected two military chiefs for the two provinces of Bordeaux and Toulouse. Colonels were chosen for each regional colloquy, with instructions to obey every order of the respective chiefs, and captains were to organise the forces of each individual church at the command of the local colonel. These forces were to be kept in readiness in case of a renewal of persecution. The ministers at Sainte-Foy were specifically instructed to see to it that the mustering was orderly and that the people did not begin rioting. Several isolated riots did occur, but the mustering was generally accomplished in good order. This form of military organisation, by "*assemblée politique*" eventually spread to every province in France. A synod at Nîmes early in 1562 applied it to that area. Other synods followed suit. In some areas these *assemblées politiques* replaced the earlier "protectors" of the Calvinist churches, who were sometimes Catholic.

In the dates cited, lies the explanation of the rapidity with which Condé was able to summon up the cadres of his army in little over a month. Most of this organisation had taken place before the massacre of Vassy and Condé's manifesto, so that when news of Vassy and the Condé declaration did arrive in the provinces, only a few weeks were needed to dispatch armed forces to Orleans or other mobilization centers.

The men of Geneva played a part in this later stage of general mobilization also, as is shown by the well-documented example in the province of Saintonge. Soon after receipt of news of the massacre of Vassy, along with special letters from Condé to La Rochefoucauld and to the churches of Saintonge, the local *assemblée politique* met in Saint-Jean-d'Angély, on March 25, 1562 before Condé had even arrived in Orleans. This assembly passed a resolution, "that in good conscience one could and must take up arms for the deliverance of the king and the queen-mother, and defense of the religion oppressed by those of Guise and their adherents against the edicts, solemnly made and published." That this *assemblée* had discovered that the king and queen-mother were captive six days before they were forced to leave Fontainebleau is rather remarkable, but Condé's letters may explain that.

On April 3, the local nobility gathered again, elected the Sire de saincte Martin de la Coudre as their chief, collected equipment, and departed, as a force of three hundred men on horse, to join the nobility of Poitou and Angoumois on the way to Orleans. Charles Léopard, the writer of several anti-clerical tracts and formerly a minister in the Lausanne territory, who had been dispatched from Geneva to a Saintonge church, was elected by the *as-*

semblée to accompany the force as their minister. His first move was to exhort the soldiers to behave.

Not all of Saintonge's nobility was willing to fight, however. Some objected to the war on both religious and political grounds. To deal with this situation a synod of the Saintonge churches was called at Saintes. Sixty ministers appeared at this meeting and passed the following resolution:

> . . . the defense undertaken by the prince by letters express from the queen against the manifest violators as much of the person of the king as of his edict very solemn and authentic, and guilty of infinite cruelties and more than execrable acts, was not only legitimate, but also very necessary.

This won most of the dubious and reluctant to the cause of religious war, though a few still refused to join. The men of Geneva must have been prominent at this synod. Léopard made a special trip back from Orleans with La Rochefoucauld to be there; so it is probable that other Geneva envoys active in churches of the area also attended. One who may have been present was Ambroise Faget, who about this time tried to persuade La Rochelle Protestants to aid Condé in some way, at the very least by permitting refugees to enter their city, and was forced to leave La Rochelle as a result.

A conclusive bit of evidence that the Calvinist church organisation was systematically used to mobilize Huguenot armies is provided by the text of an order sent by Montbrun to "the judges, chatellains, consuls, syndics or deacons of the churches" of Dauphiné. This order, dated June 28, 1562, commands some twenty-six churches of that province to send to Montbrun in Montélimar, by July 1, all the troops mobilized a month earlier, plus "all others capable of carrying arms, on pain of being hanged and strangled, their goods confiscated without hope of grace." This draconian edict reveals the thoroughness with which Huguenot leaders exploited the Geneva-created French ecclesiastical organisation.

There is also evidence that some of the provincial ministers roused their flocks to war in other ways besides encouraging nobles to mobilize. Since the sixteenth-century public so largely turned to the pulpit to have its opinions molded, a minister could easily use his respected position and his oratorical ability to make war seem desirable and respectable to the general public. An example of a minister who did just that is Jacques Ruffy, a young nobleman trained and dispatched from Geneva, who was serving in the Lyons pastoral corps in the months of the war's beginning. Word of Ruffy's activities first came to Geneva in a letter dated May 9, 1562, written by a Lyons pastor to Antoine Vincent, the printer. The pastor reported, "Several of ours were so excited in withdrawing the property of the temples that there have been already great quarrels among us . . . Several were greatly offended that one of ours carried arms publicly and the following day put himself in the pulpit." He begged Vincent to ask Calvin for advice. The letter has been preserved as part of the correspondence of the Company of Pastors; there is a secretary's note on the back referring to Calvin's response, which was immediate and violent. Calvin apparently heard further details of the disorders by word of mouth, for in a letter addressed to the Ministers of Lyons, dated May 13, he roundly scolded them for their activities at the time of the Protestant seizure of the city.

> It is not a decent act for a minister to make himself soldier or captain, but it is much worse when one leaves the pulpit to carry arms. The height of all is to come to a governor of the city with a pistol in the hand, and to menace him boasting of force and violence. . . . We have also greatly detested the (public) cry that was made by the governor and the ministers. We place in the same rank the passports and similar things. . . . (Calvin then itemizes specific acts of violence encouraged by the ministers) . . . It is true that Monsieur Ruffy is charged with all these things . . . (but Calvin also finds the other Lyons ministers partly to blame).

If Calvin's information was correct, and there is every reason to believe that it was, since some of the disturbances had been admitted in the pastor's letter to Vincent, the ministers of Lyons played an important part in the violent seizure of that metropolis from Catholic and royal authority. This seizure turned out to be of considerable importance to the Huguenot cause, when Lyons as a truly Protestant city was later to raise much of the money for the first war. However Calvin and his aids in Geneva obviously cannot be held as direct sponsors of violence in this particular instance.

The violence in Lyons was not an isolated incident: there were other ministers who failed to keep the hands of Geneva clean. When Montauban was put under siege late in 1562, its minister assigned by Geneva, Martin Tachard, led in the resistance. He accompanied the commander of the garrison on negotiation missions and constantly urged him to fight on, and when the commander was inclined to negotiate surrender anyway, Tachard and other ministers roused the people against him by preaching continued war. Tachard had more justification than Ruffy did: the ministers and the most distinguished of the faithful would have been the first to be sacrificed to the greed and savagery of the conqueror if the city had ever fallen. But Tachard's activity is an example of Geneva's influence being turned to a militarist policy in yet another area of France. No "turn the other cheek" policy here.

Augustine Marlorat, the pastor of Rouen, was accused by the enemy of preaching war. After Rouen was finally captured, Marlorat was seized, tried and convicted of encouraging sedition and rebellion. He denied all charges but did admit, "that if he preached war, it was as he had learned it in the word of God."

While these shreds of evidence are not conclusive and while there is nothing to tie these inciting activities directly to Geneva, it is clear that in some areas Calvin's envoys were responsible for stimulating war fervor and even rioting on behalf of the common cause. All three of the men mentioned above had been carefully trained and were highly regarded by Geneva. It seems probable that similar activity took place in other localities. Reports of it would naturally be scanty, for local authorities would be reluctant to volunteer news of violence to Geneva, and Geneva would not be anxious to publicize whatever reports were received.

The second great need of the revolting Huguenot armies was money, and the mustering and mobilization letters of Beza, Coligny and Condé always appealed for money as well as for men. Local churches all over France strained their resources to provide money for the Huguenot troops, the more audacious churches and those strongest in local communities even going so far as to seize Catholic church property for war uses. The Castres church, for example, seized large quantities of plate owned by the local Roman churches, and "following orders," inventoried it and sent it to Lyons for reduction into money to pay the German mercenaries being recruited by the Huguenots.

That ministerial pressure might be used to raise funds is revealed in a letter from Pierre Viret in Lyons to d'Anduze in Geneva. It seems that an official from Toulouse was willing to raise between three and four thousand soldiers in Languedoc if certain rich fugitives from Toulouse would supply the money. Viret had exhorted the refugees, then living in Lyons, to do their duty, and they had agreed to raise 18,500 écus, but a Huguenot military defeat near Lyons had scared them and many had fled to Geneva. Viret and the Toulouse minister wanted d'Anduze to ask Calvin to use his influence toward forcing the refugees to do their duty.

Calvin, himself, did not stop at indirect pressure in fund raising for the war. In a general letter to the churches of Languedoc, he appealed specifically for money to pay for the German mercenaries whom d'Andelot was at the moment trying to recruit in Germany, and he scolded the churches for past parsimony, while he reminded them of the faithful who had given up life itself for religion.

While Geneva would not sanction local rioting on behalf of the war effort, Calvin and his aids were quite willing to milk the ecclesiastical organisation they commanded for the funds necessary to wage war on a large scale. Here again, as in connection with the Amboise Conspiracy, we see that Calvin's scruples had a practical base. Rioting, which may inflame public opinion without profitable results, he rejected; businesslike financing, to lay a solid foundation for his cause, he encouraged. By no means pacifist, he accepted and supported religious war in exceedingly realistic ways.

Calvinist Self-Defense

SAMUEL MOURS

Samuel Mours, who was born in 1892, is a Protestant pastor and administrator of the Calvin Institute at the great reformer's birthplace of Noyon in Picardy. He has written a large number of works on the history of early French Protestant Churches. The following extract is taken from his general history of Protestantism in France in the sixteenth century.

We come now to the saddest period in our Protestant history, that of the Wars of Religion. And for our part, we regret that the Huguenots of that time allowed themselves to be involved in taking up arms.

The inevitable intrigues surrounding the minority of a king and the respective political ambitions of the principal protagonists (with the designs of Spain in the background) were, nearly as much as religious passion, the secret motivating forces of these wars.

On the Protestant side attitudes had changed somewhat with the adherence to the Reformation of a faction of the nobility and of several great personages in the kingdom, who were scarcely disposed to allow themselves to be maltreated without taking counter measures. Among them was a prince de Condé who was moved quite as much by ambition as by profound convictions. We have seen how in Dauphiné and elsewhere some members of the minor nobility had fled on the arrival of officers of justice. Beza's *Histoire ecclésiastique,* which recounts the sorrowful calvary of numerous churches that suffered massacres and dispersions, nowhere conceals the faults of the reformers. It tells us that at Béziers, where the Catholics displayed aggression, the Protestants "instead of going their way in humility and winning over their neighbours by the practice of what was daily preached to them, became marvellously insolent."

On the Catholic side we encounter the fixed determination of the Guises and the Triumvirs to extirpate the Protestant heresy. The ferocity of the adversaries of the Huguenots was revealed in the massacres of Cahors and Grenade and soon afterwards in those of Wassy and Sens. "It is to be noted," Agrippe d'Aubigné tells us,

From Samuel Mours, *Le Protestantisme en France au seizième siècle* (Paris, 1959), pp. 187–191, 207–209. Reprinted by permission of the author. [Editor's translation.]

that when the reformers have been put to death under the formalities of the law, however iniquitous and cruel it may be, they have offered their necks to the executioner and have in no way resisted. But when the magistrate or public authority, wearied of burnings, has handed over the knife to the people, and by the riots and great massacres that have occurred throughout France, has destroyed the venerable appearance of the law, and has had neighbour killed by neighbour to the sound of drum and trumpet, who then can forbid these unfortunates from opposing arms against arms and steel against steel, and from returning a fury lacking in justice by the condemnation of a just fury?

Could the reformers have acted in any other way? Doubtless one might have seen the indefinite continuation of the magnificent martyrology of French Protestantism, and especially the emigration, already assuming large proportions, might have been increased. But would a reformed Protestantism have survived in France? At the most, only a secret sect seems likely to have done so. To form a proper judgment on such an issue it is necessary to try to appreciate the nature of the social, political and religious structure of the French nation at this time. Such a task is not easy, but the simple fact that civil marriage was then unknown renders the clandestine existence of a large church virtually impossible. It is true that [after the revocation of the Edict of Nantes in 1685] the "church of the Desert" was able to overcome this difficulty, but the circumstances were different.

The refusal to turn itself into a political party would have probably condemned French Protestantism for a long period to the fate of Italian or Spanish Protestantism.

War is war. If the Huguenot leaders, Coligny and La Noue for instance, strove to secure discipline and morality among their soldiers, they did not always succeed. Often they were frustrated, especially when they appealed to foreign mercenaries; and more than once the Protestants allowed themselves to be involved in regrettable reprisals.

Yet though Condé apparently had no hesitation in taking up arms, it was not so with Coligny. In a well-known page Agrippe d'Aubigné tells us of the latter's hesitations and scruples:

The Admiral, having carefully weighed both sides of the question, declared one evening that he opposed resistance. Later in the night he heard his wife, Charlotte de Laval, weeping. "What is the matter?" he asked her. "Here we are sleeping in comfort," she replied, "while our friends are lying either in dungeons or in the open fields. Monsieur, my heart is bitter for the blood that our people have spilt. Their blood and your wife's voice call out to God in Heaven against you, lying in this bed, for making murderers of those who cannot prevent their own murder." Once more Coligny outlined the reasons that gave him pause — the hopelessness of popular revolts — the preponderance of strength on the enemy's side and the weakness of their own. Then he added: "Well, Madame, put your hand on your breast and see how courageous you are. Could you endure general disaster, the hatred of your enemies, the betrayals of your friends, flight and exile . . . shame, hunger and what is more, all this for your children too? . . . I give you three weeks to test your strength." His wife replied: "Your three weeks have passed already. . . . Don't let your conscience bear the weight of those who will die in the course of three weeks."

And so Coligny became one of the most outstanding of Huguenot leaders. But Condé possessed neither his moral and spiritual worth nor even his military gifts.

A single event set fire to the powder train. On 1st March 1562 the duc de Guise was passing through Vassy when he heard that some Protestants were conducting a service in a barn. If the barn in question was, as seems likely, actually situated in the town, this was an act of imprudence, for the Edict of January gave the Protestants the right to celebrate their cult outside towns only. Whatever the rights of the matter, the Duke's soldiers fell upon the congregation and massacred the participants. About sixty of them were killed and a hundred wounded. As Romier has observed, even if the Protestants were in the wrong, the massacre was a violation of all laws. Acts of "insolence" could not justify the execution of any Protestant.

The news of the massacre caused a great stir within Protestant circles in the capital. Beza went at once to the Queen to demand that justice be done. The King of Navarre, who was present at the interview, defended the duc de Guise. He provoked a fine reply from Beza: "Sire, in truth it is for the Church of God, in whose name I speak, to endure blows and not to give them. But you may also care to remember that it is an anvil that has worn out many hammers."

Despite the Queen's orders, Guise made a triumphal entry to Paris and was immediately joined by the King of Navarre. The Queen appealed to Condé and asked him to take the young King and herself under his protection. Condé acted evasively and made no effort to prevent the duc de Guise reaching Fontainebleau, where the court was located. Relying on the repeated demands of Catherine de Medici, Condé then declared the young king to be the prisoner of the Guises. On 12th April he issued a call to arms to the Protestant churches.

Many towns joined the reformed party in answer to Condé's appeal: La Rochelle, Poitiers, Le Mans, Tours, Blois, Caen, Bayeux, Rouen, Le Havre, Dieppe, Bourges and Lyons. But few of them sent troops to reinforce the army that Condé had concentrated at Orleans. Catherine de Medici attempted conciliation, but the Triumvirs insisted that the King "should neither approve nor suffer any diversity of religion in his kingdom." After other attempts at negotiation in which Condé was involved, the latter perceived the duplicity of his adversaries. By July it was clear that there could be no other outcome but war. By this time the morals of Condé's army had begun to deteriorate. Previously good order had been the rule, with prayers morning and night and all pillage forbidden, but this was replaced by license.

* * *

War occurred at the time when the evangelical movement was in the full flood of its expansion. The first war was particularly unfortunate for the churches of the northwest, of central France and in the east, as well as for those in Provence. When peace came some of the churches that had been dispersed were able to start again and rebuild the ruins, while elsewhere, in Vivarais, for example, new churches were formed. After the peace of Amboise (in 1563) several requests for pastors were still being sent to Geneva. At Gien the ministers never ceased their pastoral work throughout all the troubles and disasters of the time, and they laboured so effectively that "two fine new churches" were constructed on the outskirts of the town. The few baptismal and marriage registers that have survived allow us to conclude that even as late as 1580 Protestantism retained, wherever the circumstances were favourable, its spirit of conquest.

* * *

In every region controlled by Catholic troops, and these included royal troops until the alliance between Henry III and Henry of Navarre, not only was the reformed cult forbidden, but for most of the time (and it was the invariable rule with the League) the reformers were given the alternatives of flight (sometimes even of death) or abjuration. The periods of truce did allow certain churches to be restored, but very precariously. We know the disastrous consequences of St. Bartholomew and of various edicts of proscription.

Thus the reformers were never in a position of equality in relation to the Catholics. Not only was their fate dependent upon the always uncertain issue of success in battle, but, what was more, their existence within French society was controlled by royal edicts, of which the most favourable only accorded them a relative degree of toleration, and the others went as far as complete proscription.

When Henry IV established religious peace

one no longer saw in this exhausted nation (wrote Charles Bost) any really dense Protestant "Provinces" except on the east, south and west fringes of the Central Plateau, that is in the area where they are to be found today. Almost everywhere else the weakened communities grouped themselves in larger, scattered "Provinces," where one wept over the ruins of the past organisation.

War is always a bad thing. Certainly Coligny, La Noue and others tried to discipline their troops. Sometimes, but all too rarely, they succeeded, and we have some moving evidence of it. Was it not Beza who wrote in 1578 to the churches of Champagne?

Certainly the defence by arms has been just and necessary; but we have made such bad use of it that there is need to pray God that, if it please Him, He may never lead us back to such methods again — or that He may teach us to deal with our enemies in a more forgiving manner — or, rather, that He give us His grace to suffer all things that are sent to us, so that we may know better how to conduct so good a cause.

And yet it is necessary to recognise what was at stake — the very right of Protestantism to exist. For forty years the evangelical movement had had no other arms than the preaching of the word of God and the witness of His martyrs. If the self-interested defenders of the Roman Church — the Guises, supported by the mighty King of Spain — had not sworn to exterminate Protestantism, our country would have been spared this war and all its sorrowful consequences.

Calvin's Idealism and Indecision

N. M. SUTHERLAND

Dr. N. M. Sutherland is a lecturer at Bedford College, University of London. She is the author of *The French Secretaries of State in the Age of Catherine de Medici* (1962) and of a short study of the consequences for the *Ancien Régime* of Catherine de Medici's period of power. In the article from which this extract is taken she reconsiders the role of Calvin and several prominent Huguenot pastors in the Conspiracy of Amboise. She reexamines several points of detail in Lucien Romier's study of the same topic, and regards the conspiracy as providing insight into the origins of the wars.

THE CONSPIRACY of Amboise took place in March 1560. Although it was betrayed and suppressed and achieved nothing, it is of great historical significance for the light which it throws on the origins and nature of the French civil wars. It fixes their real origin in time, reveals the development of an opposition and provides a kind of microcosm of the greater movement which followed. This was the moment at which different groups and elements began to draw together, principally on account of their common opposition to the government. Such a negative agreement proved an unsatisfactory basis for cooperation, and the diversity of interest, which existed from the beginning, is one reason why the whole incident presents a picture of extreme confusion.

The conspiracy arose directly out of the

From N. M. Sutherland, *Calvinism and the Conspiracy of Amboise*, *History* (June, 1962), vol. XLVII, no. 160, pp. 111–138. Reprinted by permission of The Historical Association.

crisis which followed the sudden death of Henry II in July 1559. The disastrous thing about the new situation was that it superimposed a political crisis upon an already advanced religious crisis. This had the effect of confusing the issues. The religious issue had been relatively clear. Controlled by the cardinal of Lorraine, or so it was believed, Henry II had regarded the Protestants not only as heretics, but also as seditious enemies of the kingdom. Accordingly he pursued them with a savage fury, seemingly foreign to his nature, and planned their systematic extermination when released from the preoccupation of foreign war. For this reason the attempts of this distressed community to ensure its survival had slowly been sucking the protestants towards the vortex of politics and diplomacy. So long, however, as Henry's stable rule continued — albeit increasingly resented in various quarters — the affiliations of the Protestant Church with Bourbon and German princes, contracted in the search for protection, had little or no political significance. But once the accession of a youthful king precipitated a struggle for power between the persecuting house of Guise, who seized control of the court, and the supposedly pro-Protestant Bourbons, the fate of the Protestant Church was automatically involved in the outcome of the political situation. By the same token, politics and religion suddenly became inextricably entangled, to the confusion of both and the sorrow of France, for religion was not a subject on which men were prepared to compromise. As the Protestant Church was already the centre of the religious crisis, both under Henry II and under the new régime, it was naturally also the centre of attraction for those involved in the political crisis. As a result, the Protestants became a pawn in the international game of diplomacy, and were soon to be regarded as a faction in the state. Within a matter of weeks they were swept up in a mounting clamour of opposition, and their cause was rapidly embraced by many new and embarrassing recruits whose motives and interests had little in common with those of the evangelical movement.

The story of the conspiracy of Amboise reveals something of this process. But in order to understand the dual crisis from which it arose, it is necessary to examine both the previous history of the Protestant Church of Paris, and the political situation at the time of Henry's death.

. . . A gap in the pastors' correspondence leaves us with little information between October 1558 and May 1559, months during which the long war with Spain was brought to an end, and the king prepared to turn upon his Protestant subjects. Notwithstanding the unabated arrests, imprisonments and searching and sacking of houses, François de Morel, who succeeded Macar, had the courage, or temerity, to hold the first national synod in Paris in May, thus uniting the French churches in one organization at a critical moment in their history.

It was perhaps because of the presence in Paris of the Spanish representatives for the wedding of Henry's daughter Elizabeth to Philip II, that the king chose the month of June to launch his policy of extermination. Spies were placed in every *quartier* of Paris; the Protestants were outlawed and, according to Morel, judges were suborned. A goldsmith named Russanges was said to have revealed the secrets of the Paris church, and the king possessed a long list of the names of Protestants from all walks of life. These, Morel believed, he would track down systematically. It was also in June that the king arrested five members of the *parlement* who had dared to defend the Protestants, including the celebrated Anne du Bourg. The fate of du Bourg inflamed violent popular passions on both sides and, in the months which followed the death of the king, did more than anything else to exasperate the Protestants beyond the point of endurance. Calvin was quick to send his condolences on this new disaster, and to assure the church that he had tried every human means in his power to help them — he referred to his diplomatic efforts —

but the king had proudly rejected every advance. He urged them to behave quietly and peacefully, and to confound the agents of Satan by the virtue of their lives. But even Morel seems to have been growing restive. He complained that the fury of their enemies was such that it violated "tout droit divin et humain," a significant phrase, which indicates the lines upon which he, or others were thinking. He considered withdrawing from Paris because his church was virtually disrupted.

Such was the critical position of the Protestants of Paris at the beginning of July 1559. They had not, at this stage, made any demands or uttered any threats, but they were classed as traitors by the authorities, and treated like vermin by the Catholic majority of Paris. The king had sworn to destroy them and seemed likely to succeed. Yet so far Calvin's authority had prevailed upon his followers: they were a powerless minority and there was nothing they could do, or think of doing, against the Lord's anointed. But, when Henry died, the situation was radically altered, first by the hope and possibility of a drastic change of government, and when that hope faded, by the entirely new possibility, under a young king, of opposing the ministers who were held to abuse his authority. This is what the conspiracy of Amboise was concerned with, but not simply on account of the agony of the Church. On the contrary, the new political crisis partially superseded the continuing religious crisis. The separate issues remained distinct in theory, while becoming entangled in practice.

. . . Not least of those who turned to Navarre and tried to galvanize him into action in the crisis of 1559 were the Protestants of Paris. Morel and the consistory wasted no time in sending La Roche-Chandieu to meet him. He had gone, Morel told Calvin, to remind Navarre of his rights and inform him of their will and that of "toute la noblesse" lest he should neglect such an opportunity. It would be interesting to know what Morel meant by "toute la noblesse," for the phrase is clearly significant. Early in August Morel received Calvin's explicit instructions for dealing with the situation caused by Henry's death. Unfortunately these instructions are not available and our knowledge of what they contained is derived from Morel's reply. Calvin's purpose was that Navarre should be induced to hurry to court to assume the position due to his rank as first prince of the blood, and forthwith inaugurate a policy favourable to the Protestants. It was not that Calvin had any real confidence in Navarre but that in the new circumstances occasioned by the king's death, he was too important to ignore. It is clear from the correspondence that Calvin had some elaborate plan for placing Navarre in power, and also that this was an adaptation of a previous plan, already contrived with certain German princes in cooperation with François Hotman, professor of law at Strasbourg, and their mutual friend Jean Sturm, rector of the academy there. But it is not clear what the plan was. The implication would appear to be that Calvin's instructions envisaged a veritable *coup d'état,* backed by foreign help, to put Navarre in his legitimate place at the head of the government. It is true that Calvin later referred to the permissibility of the use of force, at the same time deprecating bloodshed or the risk of bloodshed. One must, however, presume, in the case of Navarre, that he was taking at least a calculated risk. The contradiction is not easily resolved. In a letter of 2 September to his friend Bullinger of the church of Zurich, Hotman referred to this matter quite plainly. Lamenting the way in which Navarre had miserably disappointed everybody's hopes, he said, "If you only knew . . . what conditions were offered him, what help was placed at his disposal." Although Calvin constantly preached patience and obedience, it is also clear from his own correspondence that he did envisage the use of force, if necessary, to install Navarre in power at the end of 1560. The explanation of the tenacity with which he pursued this purpose and declined to support any other lies in his political philosophy. To Calvin, it was only through the agency of Navarre and his legitimate claim to power that any alteration of the government in France could lawfully be undertaken.

In accordance with Calvin's instructions, and in order to arouse Navarre more thoroughly "et lui enlever toute crainte," Morel himself set out to meet him, arriving after the departure of Chandieu.

Morel worked on Navarre by every means he could and found him a little better disposed towards them than previously. The trouble was that he was being frightened by three of his own councillors who were acting as agents of the Guises—Montluc, the bishop of Mende, and d'Escars—who, Morel was convinced, were paid "pour l'enerver." This is confirmed by La Planche, who makes the same observation. Morel reminded Navarre that the government of France had been placed within his grasp by divine intervention, and that he might now assume power with the assent of all the orders—by which he meant the Estates General. Everyone, he said, was sick of the rapacity and arrogance of the Guises. The situation could only worsen if they were allowed to fortify themselves in power, and the calamities of the church could surely not be forgotten. "Finally," wrote Morel significantly, in his report to Calvin, "in the event of someone barring his way, I explained to him how the adversaries could be reduced to silence, relying principally upon what I had seen in the instructions." As Morel was returning to Paris, his colleague La Rivière brought him another, similar set of instructions from Hotman, containing certain useful additions. Faced with what was apparently a definite proposition, Navarre began to hedge, saying that he would assert his rights in every way he could. If he succeeded, then he could easily help the afflicted. But if the injustice of his adversaries prevailed, he would return home again as quickly as possible. Stung by the ensuing torrent of Morel's reproaches, Navarre enquired of him how it was that Calvin disposed of such power ("un pareil pouvoir"), and upon what princes he relied for help. Morel evidently did not know for certain and replied—perhaps a little pointedly—that Calvin never made frivolous promises. Assuming that it must be the German princes, Navarre declared that they were full of promises, but that when it came to the point, they seldom fulfilled them. Thus, Morel went on, "having neither accepted nor refused the proposition which I took him," Navarre enjoined him to secrecy, saying that they would continue the conversation in Paris. It was therefore not yet possible to say what could be hoped for him.

Morel, however, knew Navarre, and there was little doubt in his mind as to what the outcome would be. In the same letter, therefore, he asked Calvin whether, in the case of Navarre's defection, there were not some other means of delivering the church from her present sufferings. He was aware, he said, that Calvin considered prayers and holy offices their principal means of succour. But he also pointed out that apart from the plan involving Navarre—which he clearly already considered abortive—Calvin had not proposed any "moyens moins sublimes." Morel himself went on to make a suggestion. When a minor ascended the throne, he said, according to the law of France the Estates General ought to be summoned to appoint tutors and councillors for the duration of the minority. Thus, as it was licit to summon the Estates, Morel queried whether Navarre alone had the right to do this? Could the demand not be made by anybody, and, if refused, would it not be just for anybody to take up arms against the monopoly of tyrants and of their small faction? The fact that Morel dared to raise the possibility of using force—in what he took to be permissible political circumstances—adds weight to the deduction that Calvin himself had sanctioned the use of force in support of Navarre. Unfortunately we do not know whether these were Morel's own ideas, or whether he was reporting discussions which were taking place around him. If the latter, then this report is probably among the first rumblings of Amboise, heard only five weeks after Henry's death.

. . . The severity of the persecution endured by the Paris Protestants in the summer of 1558 fully accounts for Morel's efforts to obtain help and for his warnings of impending trouble. He reported to Calvin that the cardinal's fury knew no limits. Scarcely a week passed without arrests, the sacking of houses, burnings at the stake, or someone being torn limb from limb. Even more serious, following the example of Paris, there was an upsurge of popular hatred against the Protestants all over France. La Planche said that Paris resembled a conquered city. Many Protestants had fled, their empty houses were sacked and their property stolen. Abandoned children roamed the streets and people were afraid to help them. Obscene libels appeared against the Protestants, who were blamed for all the anti-Guise publications. Early in September they suffered a further act of treachery and their houses and meeting places were revealed to the authorities. Morel's own name had been betrayed, and his features and clothing described. He hardly dared venture outside. A mass of arrests resulted, and it was almost impossible to do anything to help the prisoners or to send them money. Some were exposed to heatstroke, without food or water. Some were confined without light or air, breathing in the exhalations of human excrement, and others were locked in torture cells, in which they could neither sit, lie nor stand. To Morel, their fate was worse than that of burning at the stake, and there was not even a show of bringing them to justice. Sixty *commissaires* were appointed to make house-to-house searches in Paris, and Morel believed that the policy of extermination would soon be successful. This was why he tried to arrange for a mass emigration, whether to England or to Strasbourg.

The betrayal of the Protestant meeting places resulted in a raid on certain houses in the faubourg Saint-Germain, beginning with the house of one Visconte, where the authorities hoped to catch a group of Protestants eating meat on a Friday. Accordingly, the house was surrounded at dinner time, but the occupants offered a fierce resistance and most of them escaped. On the same occasion, Hercule Coiffart, the bailly of Saint-Aignan, was arrested in a neighbouring house and found to be in possession of incriminating papers containing remonstrances addressed to the king and the Estates General, concerning both religion and political affairs. These documents were alleged to be "divinement bien faicts." This aroused speculation as to their provenance since they could only have been drafted by educated persons of intellectual distinction, and could not be attributed to common rebels. The discovery of these documents may very well be another pointer to the origins of the conspiracy. The date of this incident is not well attested, but is alleged to have been a Friday in August. It could therefore have been as early as the 4th. It is worth bearing in mind that there may have been some connection between the existence of such papers in the possession of a group of Protestants in Paris, and Morel's letter to Calvin of 15 August in which he made his remarks about the Estates General and reported on his correspondence with Catherine. On the other hand it might be more correct to relate the concern which he expressed in mid-August to his journey to Vendôme — which probably occurred between about the 4th and 10th — rather than to events in Paris.

Whatever the truth of this matter, it is evident that opposition was mounting and patience expiring. "Plusieurs," wrote La Planche, "se faschoyent de la patience chrestienne . . . n'obeissant rien moins en cela qu'à leurs ministres," a statement which, in fact, bears out Morel's warning. People began, said La Planche, to rise up against the Guises, as usurping tyrants. A demand arose for the Bourbon princes to assume control and summon the Estates General, because of a widespread belief that the Guises meant to usurp the kingdom. This was not hysterical gossip, but the considered opinion of sober observers. We have already seen that Morel believed it. So did de Bèze. Everyone, said La Planche, was therefore forced to "penser à son particulier," and, unable to endure such oppression any longer "commencèrent à se rallier ensemble pour regarder à quelque juste défense." Such things, he said, were generally "proposées et débatues ès compagnies." More specific than this it is not possible to be.

These were the circumstances, political and religious, in which the conspiracy of Amboise had its roots, though its precise origins are veiled in obscurity and the evidence is entangled with that relating to other plots. There are strong grounds for believing that the plot passed through different stages before reaching the final form in which it took place, probably on account of a struggle for influence between the different elements involved. In the words of La Planche, these different elements comprised those who were moved by "un droict zèle" to serve God, their prince and their country, those who were moved by ambition and a desire for change, and those who were stung by a craving for revenge for injuries received at the hands of the Guises.

. . . La Planche clearly states that the initiative in the conspiracy came from an unspecified "compagnie." These people were agreed upon the necessity of seeking some legitimate form of defence "pour remettre sus l'ancien et légitime gouvernement du royaume," an objective which, at that stage, was political, limited and lawful. This group — not inconceivably those in possession of the documents "divinement bien faicts" — is said to have consulted the most learned jurists and theologians of France and Germany. As a result, it was claimed that they might legitimately oppose the government usurped by the Guises, and take up arms, in case of resistance, provided the princes of the blood, or one of them would lead the enterprise. At this stage, La Planche went on, Condé was approached ("sollicité d'entendre à ces affaires"). The prince, he says, considered the matter carefully, and requested certain prudent and suitable persons to examine and enquire into the case against the Guises, in order to see what could and ought to be done, in all good conscience and for the benefit of the king and the commonwealth. It was the difficulty of implementing their objectives which turned the movement into a conspiracy. As the king was entirely controlled by the Guises, it was impossible to petition the council. It followed that the Guises must somehow be arrested and the Estates General assembled. The problem was how and by whom this could be done ("à qui attacher la sonnette"). It was at this point that the services of the leader La Renaudie were enlisted, and, according to La Planche, it was La Renaudie himself who proffered his services. Romier, without saying why, supposed that Chandieu presented La Renaudie to Condé. But we know that La Renaudie had been in touch with the Paris Protestants for at least eighteen months, and may well have been involved in the discussions from the start. He was connected with Navarre, who summoned him in March 1558, and was possibly even one of his servants. It is therefore absurd to suggest that Condé only met La Renaudie through the agency of Chandieu in the summer of 1559, more especially since La Renaudie was *persona non grata* to Calvin.

. . . There is no reason to reject this version of La Planche: it is the most authoritative we have. It makes no mention of Chandieu, or of Morel, whom Romier also ignored. What then was the position of these pastors? Unfortunately it remains a matter for speculation. We know that they were both concerned, at some point, with discussions relating to a change of government. We also know that, faced with a choice between resistance and extermination, they desired some solution less sublime than that of prayer alone. We do not know who were the learned men who approved, or were alleged to have approved, the conspiracy, but it is quite possible that Morel and Chandieu may have assented to the original purpose—"remettre sus l'ancien et légitime gouvernement du royaume." Calvin himself approved of this. Bearing in mind, therefore, that the intention was not to organize a rebellion, but to devise a means of legitimate opposition, it is even conceivable that Chandieu may have been among those who approached Condé. It is true that he had been connected with Condé for some time and had a brother, Bertrand, in the prince's service. But further than this one cannot go. In the absence of proper evidence—and Romier produces none—it is impossible to agree that Chandieu, or any of the pastors, helped to organize the conspiracy in the form in which it took place. It is almost certainly a failure to make this distinction between the original purpose and what actually occurred, which accounts both for the claim that the conspiracy was approved by those consulted, and for the fact that the pastors are said to have been implicated in the final scheme.

Chandieu's position is nevertheless bewildering, since late in September or early in October he went to Geneva to discuss the conspiracy with Calvin and the Company of Pastors. . . . [His] mission raises various problems but proves only one thing: that he knew something of what was going on and, by inference, the general nature of the conspiracy. It does not, as Romier appears to assume, prove his complicity. . . . What little we know for certain about [it] comes from a letter of 16 April 1561 from Calvin to Coligny—although he concealed the identity of Chandieu—and from information recorded in Geneva in the course of a libel case in which Calvin, de Bèze and Chandieu were accused of complicity in the conspiracy. Jean Morély, Chandieu's accuser, alleged before the *seigneurie* of Geneva that the original plans ("premiers propos") were "si equitables et tellement fondés en la Parolle de Dieu qu'il semblait la chose se debvoir entreprendre." Thus, Morély went on, Chandieu went to Geneva to discuss the matter with Calvin and the pastors, and subsequently informed the French churches that they had approved the enterprise. One must either assume that Morély's evidence was hopelessly garbled, or else that the report is incomplete, for the statement, as it stands, does not make sense. For his part, Chandieu denied having told the French churches that the ministers of Geneva approved the enterprise, "ainsi qu'elle a esté executée"; he knew that they did not. Here we have at least one clear statement amidst so much that is obscure, and there is no reason to doubt its veracity. In answer to another question, Chandieu said that he had spoken to Calvin of the tyranny of the Guises and of the need to establish a government of "the prince"—it is not clear which prince is intended—in view of the king's minority, and in accordance with the laws of France. These were, presumably, the "premiers propos," held to be in accordance with the word of God. According to Chandieu's evidence, Calvin replied that this was a purely civil matter, and that if Navarre and the Estates General combined to restore order there was no objection to the Protestants lending their support ("il ne trouvait mauvais que les fideles . . . fussent du nombre").

It is apparent, however, that Chandieu must—though not necessarily on the same occasion—have said more than the evidence states, and advanced some actual plan, since Calvin, in his evidence, claimed to have given Chandieu many reasons why the enterprise, "telle qu'elle estoit," was not based on the word of God. But if, Calvin went on, it were a question of supporting Navarre in an attempt to reestablish the proper order laid down by the laws of France, it would be permissible so long as it were done without the effusion of blood—a new development in Calvinist thought. Calvin here expressed himself ambiguously and without indicating the nature of the support he was prepared to sanction. The letter to Coligny of April 16, 1561 is easier to follow. . . . From this we infer that there was a general discussion between Calvin and Chandieu on the legitimacy and the means of resistance. Realizing, Calvin said, that many people were deeply involved in plans for resistance, he gave a categorical answer that the idea — precisely which idea is not stated — must be abandoned. He tried to show that it was not founded in the word of God, and also that it was foolish, and could not hope to succeed. Chandieu, he said, disputed his answer, "voir avec quelque couleur," because there was no question of taking action either against the king or the royal authority, but only of calling for a government in conformity with the law. Meanwhile, if nothing were done, a horrible massacre was hourly expected, which would put an end to the reformed religion. Calvin says he replied — referring presumably to the project — that if a single drop of blood were shed, then rivers of blood would flow throughout Europe. Thus, he maintained, it was preferable that all the Protestants should die a hundred deaths, than that the Church should incur so frightful a responsibility. Nevertheless, Calvin again stated that if the princes of the blood, together with the *parlement,* demanded support for their rights in the common interest, it would be legitimate for all good subjects to go to their assistance. Here again, Calvin used an evasive expression — "de leur prêter main forte." In this version, the *parlement* is substituted for the Estates General, and there is no reservation about the avoidance of bloodshed. The questioner then asked him, Calvin continued, whether the same plan were permissible if only one of the princes took part, an obvious reference to Condé. The answer again was an absolute negative, and Calvin believed that the project would therefore be abandoned. This could be taken to imply that plans for the conspiracy had not yet been completed, that Chandieu was not very well informed, or that Calvin had had an inflated conception of his own influence; certainly he regretted his loss of influence in the same letter to Coligny.

As far as Chandieu is concerned, the evidence is still inconclusive. It implies a certain degree of sympathy with the conspirators on account of his fears for the Church; but this is in keeping with Calvin's own support of the "premier propos." We may deduce from Calvin's evidence that Chandieu must have mentioned Condé, and Romier assumes that Chandieu pleaded the cause of the conspirators, that is to say, supported the plans which were actually carried out. To this it may be objected that we neither know what Chandieu said, nor whether he pleaded or merely reported. We only know for certain that Condé was mentioned and that Calvin thought the proposition plausible, but inexpedient. The enigma remains, but the most likely explanation is that Chandieu described a plan proposing the substitution of Condé for Navarre, who was even then preparing for his journey to Spain. This would have been a strictly practical adaptation of Calvin's own plan. Many people, and perhaps Chandieu himself, must have thought the difference between the first and the second prince of the blood no more than a juridical quibble. Indeed, it is doubtful whether Calvin himself attached much importance to the distinction. It is clear that his absolute refusal to sanction whatever plan was suggested proceeded more from his fear of the consequences than from any theoretical consideration. Similarly, his violent disapproval of the enterprise which followed was based partly on contempt for La Renaudie and his methods, and partly on a well-founded conviction that anything so foolhardy was sure to be disastrous. It is impossible to explain this change in Calvin's attitude since the time of the conference at Vendôme, and Chandieu's mission to Geneva tends to suggest that it may have come as a surprise to him.

While Chandieu was in Geneva, it seems likely that La Renaudie had begun to organize the conspiracy, and it is probably correct to assume, not that Chandieu failed to make a truthful report when he returned, but that he arrived too late to influence events. Condé, and military-minded gentlemen like La Renaudie, were clearly not going to wait upon Calvin's permission.

Jean du Barry, seigneur de La Renaudie, sometimes known as La Forest, was a gentleman from Périgord. He was energetic, persuasive, embittered and unprincipled. He harboured a sense of injustice because of past troubles, and against the Guises in particular for the recent execution of his kinsman de Buy. He evidently had useful connections, and belonged to that section of society to which military adventures were a normal occupation. La Renaudie received a mandate from Condé and proceeded, with more celerity than prudence, to organize what was, in effect if not in intention, a military coup. Thus the initiative passed into the hands of the country gentry or lesser nobility.

. . . From the military point of view, the conspiracy was organized at Nantes, and the meeting [which La Renaudie had summoned at Nantes on February 1, 1560] is interesting for its curiously scrupulous deliberations which appear to reflect the restraining influence of those who sought some effective means of opposition without becoming rebels. We do not know who attended the meeting, but "un bon nombre de noblesse et du tiers estat de toutes les provinces" are said to have been there. It was claimed that they represented a spontaneous and legitimate gathering of the Estates. La Renaudie began by addressing the meeting at length, principally on the government of the Guises. He spoke of the decisions of the learned men who had been consulted — presumably alleging their approval — and asked whether the assembly would agree to support a prince or his lieutenant in an attempt to seize the tyrants, assemble the Estates and provide the king with a suitable council. It was agreed that the project was just and necessary, provided there was to be no attack on the royal authority or the state. An oath was taken to this effect and La Renaudie revealed his mandate from Condé. Condé was to declare himself and petition the king and council, but only after the Guises had been safely arrested.

The meeting then proceeded to consider how and when to carry out their intentions, how many men to use, which captains would command the forces and who should act as advisers to the leader or his lieutenant. The final details of this exploit were to be decided on the spot and nearer the time, by those responsible for its execution. It was formally stated that to do more than arrest the Guises would be unlawful. The assembly then appointed a council of "certain personnages de toutes les provinces." This council fixed the date of the enterprise for 10 March (it was subsequently delayed by about a week) and decided that five hundred gentlemen, drawn from all the provinces, should be assembled. This company was to assist the leader to capture the Guises, and a captain was appointed to command each local or provincial contingent. Finally, it was decided that men and money must be raised so that if the company of five hundred met with any resistance, they could defend themselves ("la force demeureroit au chef"), until they had been able to establish a legitimate government and bring the tyrants to justice. The meeting then dispersed, everyone to make appropriate preparations. La Renaudie went to Paris to see Condé, and to raise men, arms and horses.

Shortly after the assembly at Nantes, the conspiracy was betrayed, information reaching the government from several different sources. As a result, the movement collapsed, and many of those involved were killed or arrested as they gathered in small bands in the neighbourhood of Amboise. La Renaudie himself was killed on 18 March in the forest of Châteaurenault, and his secretary La Bigne, was captured. Much of what is known about the nature of the movement is based on the documents taken from La Bigne. Among them was a statement of objectives opening with the oath of loyalty to the king. The purpose, the document declared, was to put an end to the government of the Guises and, by means of a legitimate assembly of the Estates, to re-establish the ancient customs of France. The only reason why they appeared in arms for this purpose was because they feared that the Guises would accuse them of sedition and employ the king's forces against them. A second document seized from La Bigne was a separate remonstrance, addressed to the king. It contained an article defending those Protestants who had voluntarily joined the movement, on the grounds that it was a political matter concerning the laws and the service of the king. Had it been otherwise, the document stated, they would never have become involved because of their principle of obedience, already openly declared in their confession of faith. For this reason, they condemned and disclaimed all "seditieux et perturbateurs de l'ordre de justice." They hoped to present the confession of faith to the Estates General, in order to obtain some remission of the persecution which they suffered at the hands of the Guises. This apology, however, had no effect, and the Guises hastened to blame the Protestants and declare that they had taken up arms against the king. In reply, they published a further remonstrance. It was couched in similar terms, explained the loyal and political motives behind the conspiracy, and again insisted that the Protestants involved had not taken up arms for the sake of religion.

If the conspiracy of Amboise had succeeded, it would have been a bloodless, or almost bloodless *coup d'état,* accomplished by the lesser nobility, and Calvin and the Churches would have rejoiced. Though the story is confused and the evidence is often vague, it seems reasonably clear that this bloodless *coup* is what was really intended, at least by the more responsible of those involved. The movement began with an unspecified group of people, probably comprising at least a proportion of intellectuals. They were evidently Protestants in or around Paris, but we do not know whether any of them were members of the Paris church. Their original purpose was to consider by what legitimate means they could end the tyranny of the Guises and replace them by a government of the royal princes. This, we may safely assume, corresponds to the "premiers propos," or the allegedly just and reasonable intentions. This was of immediate concern to all protestants because their very existence was threatened by the régime. For this same reason the churches were accused of complicity in the act of insubordination which ultimately occurred. These original objectives were a legitimate concern of the pastors of Paris, who knew that Calvin himself had tried to replace the Guises by the King of Navarre. When this project was thwarted by Navarre himself, it was natural, in the midst of such fearful persecution, that they should have desired some alternative solution. We do not know whether they took any initiative in this matter, or merely reported the ideas of others, but Morel and Chandieu each put forward a suggestion. Morel proposed to elevate the importance of the Estates General above that of the first prince of the blood, and call an assembly without his authority. If this were resisted, then he urged that it would surely be just to take up arms. The plan expounded — though not necessarily supported — by Chandieu was evidently that of substituting Condé for Navarre, an adaptation of Calvin's own original proposal.

These propositions were well within the spirit of Calvinism, though not, as it happened, the interpretation placed by Calvin on his own work. Neither of them was favourably received, and there is nothing to show that the pastors played any part in what followed. It is therefore impossible to agree with historians who fail to distinguish between the early and the later stages of the movement and, as a result, allege or infer that Chandieu was guilty of complicity in the actual conspiracy. It is true that he is alleged to have produced an anti-Guise pamphlet in October 1559, but the theme of this relates to the "premiers propos," and is not contrary to the spirit of Calvinism. There seems to be no reason for suspecting Chandieu at this stage, since he and his colleagues evidently managed to restrain the sorely tried Protestants of Paris, none of whom is known to have been present at Amboise.

Calvin's own proposal having failed, he would accept no other: to him there was no legitimate alternative. But, unable to compromise, he was equally unable to convince all French Protestants of their duty to suffer and to die. . . . It was no fault of Calvin that religion and politics had become disastrously entangled in France. But because he offered no material solution, he was forced to watch, with impotent distress, events which quickly proved the accuracy of his fears. Control of the Protestant movement passed from the disciplined evangelists into the hands of politicians and extremists, and the churches were forced into the struggle which ensued.

A Dissident Nobility Under the Cloak of Religion

LUCIEN ROMIER

Lucien Romier (1885–1944) was a successful journalist and politician as well as being the most distinguished historian writing on the Wars of Religion in the first quarter of this century. A graduate in arts, he was also trained as an archivist-paleographer and was a diplomate of the *Ecole pratique des hautes études*. His reputation as an historian may, perhaps, outlast that which he acquired as the editor of the *Figaro* and as a minister of state in the years 1940–1943. His study of the reign of Henry II, written to determine the political origins of the civil wars, was followed by his book on France on the eve of the conflicts and by further works on the conspiracy of Amboise and on politics at the court of Charles IX. Although some aspects of his account have been questioned (his interpretation of the conspiracy of Amboise is criticized by Dr. Sutherland in the article used in the preceding extract), he remains the foremost historian of the politics of the early part of the period. Political interpretation is his principal concern, but, as the following extract shows, he is continually aware of the social implications in his narrative.

MICHELET has observed how few were the members of the nobility — three at most — who appeared in Crespin's *Martyrology* in the forty-year period 1515–1555. In fact it was not until the year 1557, just at the time when the Châtillon and Bourbon families began to join the Reformation, that the new ideas perceptibly influenced the nobility, a trend that owed much to feminine propaganda. Between the death of Henry II and the advent of civil war the number of noble converts steadily increased. We are not here concerned with finding the political and social causes of this movement, but rather with showing how the form of the Protestant communities was modified by it.

The spread of "heresy" within the military class was too immediately important to the fate of the monarchy for the royal government not to show concern. Indeed, it was a subject much discussed at the court of Francis II. In the last months of 1559 pessimistic observers claimed "that the

From Lucien Romier, *Les Protestants français à la veille des Guerres civiles* in *Revue Historique*, tome CXXIV, 1917, pp. 254–263. Reprinted by permission of the Presses Universitaires de France. [Editor's translation.]

flower of the army was most severely infected, both foot and horse and the greater part of the nobility." At the time of the Tumult of Amboise the Cardinal de Lorraine himself appeared overwhelmed by the Protestant problem. He declared that every day he encountered such sympathies among the principal ministers, their servants and their relations, so that one no longer knew "where to turn or whom to trust." Such was the anxiety of the Guises that they sent spies into the provinces "to discover and report what each little assembly was doing." A contemporary said that in November 1560 the King's uncles by marriage had in their possession "a list of more than two thousand gentlemen of the reformed religion." This might well be an accurate figure.

The dissident nobility formed family and regional groups which did not always correspond to the development of the churches. The trend of the seigneurs towards Protestantism usually followed the bonds of parentage or vassality. In Picardy and Brittany the Reformation won over many of the lesser nobility without seriously involving the rest of the population. However, the evidence on this point is sometimes contradictory. At court in the spring of 1560 there seemed to be alarm at the defection of the country nobility, notably in Gascony, Brittany, Lyonnais, Provence and also Ile-de-France, where the military nobility was poor. More reliance may be placed on a report of a familiar of the Bourbons, Pedro d'Albret, who at Nérac was well placed to know his patron's intrigues. In a secret report to Philip II, Pedro stated that "in all Guyenne, Touraine, Poitou, Lyonnais, Agenais, Dauphiné, Parisis etc. there are few nobles who do not deem it an honour to belong to the sect." This last aspect is exaggerated, but the general view seems a correct one. By Guyenne must be understood almost the whole country south-west of the Loire. In the area near Niort alone in November 1560 the Count du Lude feared a rising of eight to nine hundred men-at-arms in the Bourbon cause. Contemporary witnesses made no mention of the Norman nobility because it abstained, probably under Coligny's influence, from taking part in La Renaudie's plot, but in the following year, 1561, the Norman delegates were to be seen taking the leadership among the Huguenot nobility at the Estates General and the Colloquy of Poissy. The nobles from the Chartres area acted similarly.

The religious claims of the nobility at the Estates of Orléans seem rather confused. The *cahiers* of the order were drawn up separately by three groups of provinces which had not succeeded in achieving a common submission, and they bear witness to the diversity and incoherence of opinion. But generally the nobility showed greater bitterness towards the church, and in these terms were far more critical than were the deputies of the Third Estate. Isolated in this way, some of the nobles dared to make a public demonstration on behalf of the new religion by submitting a formal request. *Cahiers* are to be found containing demands that "the judges do no violence to the consciences of individuals" that "no one should be obliged by force to enter the flock of Jesus Christ, but that the sword of the word of God may be used as the only means of drawing to Him those who are called and chosen to believe." Moreover, the right to open temples and hold assemblies was claimed. Finally, when the spokesman for the clergy treated the Protestants as shameless criminals and asked the King to banish them, the orator for the nobility, speaking for the majority of his order, demanded the retraction of these insults. Some of the deputies had evidently received a set of over-riding instructions, but we cannot explain here why these instructions were not completely fulfilled. In truth, if there were many members of the nobility who came to Orléans animated with the wish to "protest," the majority it seems had no very clear idea of the nature of the Reformation nor of the legal status that it was advisable to give it. Some months later the representatives of the nobility of the Estates of Pontoise showed themselves much more aware of the issues, and nearly all of them associated themselves with the proceedings of the pastors on the occasion of the Colloquy of Poissy.

An obvious aspect of the *cahiers* was the desire of the nobles to safeguard or to restore their ancient feudal rights, whether in the choice or presentation of nominees to benefices or in the control and use of church revenues. The uncertain state of society and the poverty from which the nobility by descent suffered at that time, were evident in the tone with which they denounced the wealth of the church, and even banned the making of offerings, "whatever their kind may be." They claimed complete freedom in making contributions at religious services. The majority also demanded slackening of the rules for monastic life, a lowering of the age for novices and the suppression of the gifts accompanying the taking of vows. Such demands suited the heads of families, who could thereby more easily place their children in monasteries and disinherit them, where they were too numerous or could not be adequately dowered. In short, the nobility were thinking of their own interest and were not particularly concerned with bringing it into accord with any precise doctrine.

It cannot be denied that selfish passion and sometimes unrestrained greed persuaded many of the nobility and captains to join the Protestants. Study of the social background would reveal that the ruined heirs of feudal families merely awaited a chance to find a breach in the fortress of the royal power and to reconstitute their fortunes by any means they found to hand. The wealth of the church, very often based on former gifts by the nobility, seemed a standing offence to this impoverished class. Almost all the nobles who became Huguenots were descended from old lines that had been uprooted by "new nobles" and middle class men.

On this point no single witness was mistaken. Evidence from Catholic, Protestant and *Politique* sources is in agreement. Pedro d'Albret who, as we have said, was a familiar of the Bourbons and well placed to know the basis of the movement of 1560, declared "The nobles are promised all the wealth of the church." At the time of the Tumult of Amboise, bands of the lesser nobility were to be seen in such poor provinces as Brittany, scouring the countryside to enlist gentlemen, soldiers and adventurers. "They promise," wrote the Sieur de Bouillé,

> to give them money, arms and horses, and they tell them that, if they are willing to go with them, they will make them all rich, that they will pillage all the churches and rich establishments, that all Frenchmen are already of their religion, and that they are going to create the same state of affairs in Brittany.

These were very odd reformers, whose detestable influence the chancellor de L'Hospital never ceased to condemn. "Several," he wrote,

> pretend to assume the mantle of religion, however godless they may be, and indeed they are more like atheists than men of religion. Among them there are ruined persons who have consumed and expended all that they possess and who can only live from the trouble that is rife throughout the kingdom and from the substance of others. There are soldiers and other men of poor status who have joined the reformed religion.

It is hardly necessary to speculate on the theological preferences of such a nobility whose gross ignorance, in this century of the Renaissance, was denounced by the people themselves!

But to discredit all the members of the nobility who supported the Reformation would be to commit an error and an injustice. Questions of sincerity are nearly always insoluble and can only be discussed in terms of individual conscience. Members of the same family belonging to one party might obey quite different motives. The Catholic curé Claude Haton cited the example of the two Esternay brothers who became Protestants. One was a brutal and vindictive example of the type that lived extravagantly, the other showed himself, in contrast, to be "sympathetic, a generous alms-giver, very charitable and gracious, never proud and ready to help all comers."

It is rather less important to estimate the ulterior designs of such and such a notable Huguenot, or group of country nobility, than it is to know how the dissident nobility succeeded in exercising so great an influence upon the reformed churches in the period preceding the civil war, and how the army was constituted that was to be raised on Condé's orders in 1562. The explanation should take account of the social reconciliation which occurred in the middle of the sixteenth century between the nobility and the poor classes at the expense of the church and the monarchy. One observation will suffice to show the cause of this phenomenon. The royal administration was losing its personal character and becoming more and more mechanical and fiscal, and the benefices of the church were deserted by nonresident clerics. Thus humble people sought a defender among the nobles, who nearly always resided on their lands. This is what explains the rapid development of the system of "protectors" among the Protestant communities.

The reformers lived, as much individually as collectively, under a régime of permanent insecurity. In the shelter of the small towns they had less to fear from the edicts of persecution (since the royal officials, as we shall see, noticeably weakened their rigour) than they had from the violent acts of their fellow citizens. The Catholic or "atheist" populace jeered at those who held secret assemblies. They welcomed, and spread on their own account, the most unfavourable stories, which circulated in the very suburbs where the conventicles were hidden. It is easy to imagine how suspect must have appeared the nightly comings and goings of strangers or of members of the upper classes through urban back streets and on the fields outside the towns. From such reactions resulted the outcries, the stone-throwings, the brawls, the tumults and the burnings. From Easter 1561 these incidents became much more frequent and more serious. The bishops and the curés then tried to rouse those of the Catholic faith by preaching. Some did so with moderation, and even with gentleness, but more often a free hand was left to the monks, who from their pulpits set out to excite popular passions against the Huguenots. There emerged "an astounding hatred" and a stronger and stronger inclination on the part of the adversaries to "cut each other's throats." The massacres began.

We have seen that the communities, in so far as the wealth of the faithful had allowed them, had at first taken pains to conceal their places of worship in order to escape insults and violence. But towards 1560 it was scarcely possible for them to hide themselves, and the mass of Protestants sought open recognition. New conditions, as we have seen, obliged them to worship in public and to worship in arms. Who could then organize and assure the protection of services if it were not the local nobility, who took advantage of their asserted right to be always armed and escorted?

In the course of the years 1560 and 1561 most of the Protestant churches placed themselves in this way under guard of a "protector," either a great seigneur or a simple country gentleman. The consistories and the synods encouraged this movement, which developed very rapidly in the south with a regional or even a provincial character. Henceforth there was no community however small, which was not defended in some way or other. Such an organisation did not everywhere conceal political designs, since certain churches, before choosing a protector, went so far as to request approval from the royal officials, apparently without any sense of irony. Burie, lieutenant to the government of Guyenne, received in this way a request from the Protestants of Rouergue who were alarmed by the news that "several persons, and particularly the priests, have begun to form armed bands who have taken an oath and have resolved to massacre all those who profess to attend the assemblies."

Among the noble protectors of the churches a true hierarchy was fatally and inevitably established in accordance with feudal custom. In some provinces this hierarchy soon became formally acknowledged. From the month of November 1560 the synod of Clairac, directed by Boisnormand, the friend of the Bourbons, approved the formation of religious and military cadres for the communities of Guyenne. The province was divided into seven colloquies, and the captains, under the nominal control of the churches, could regard the armed faithful as their soldiers. The synod of Sainte-Foy in Agenais completed these cadres in the following year. It was then decided "by the gentlemen who were present" that two general leaders should be chosen and named protectors, one for the Bordeaux area and the other with jurisdiction in Toulouse. The colloquies of these two districts would in addition have at their heads "colonels" to whom the particular "captains" of the churches would be subordinate,

> it being established that nothing could be done or arranged by these captains without the authority of the colloquy, nor by the colonels without the wish or command of the chief of the province.

The purpose given this organisation was to "lead towards His Majesty the forces of the churches" in case of need, and also to "provide for defence."

Now this happened six months before the first civil war, on the morrow of the Colloquy of Poissy, in the period when Théodore de Bèze and Coligny were sincerely trying to reconcile the Protestants with Catherine de Medici, and promising her to respect royal authority and public order.

It is doubtful whether, outside Guyenne, Languedoc, Provence, and Dauphiné, the organisation of the protectors had attained a similar development so quickly, but it was at least established everywhere in outline when the war broke out in 1562. Thenceforth, the dissident nobility relied not only on their ancient rights and class interests, but also on the living strength of the communities, which were ensnared, whether consciously or not, in a net from which they could no longer escape. Condé then assumed the title of "Protector General of the Churches of France," a title which had a very exact meaning.

It is quite probable that the pastors collaborated in this work in all innocence and without foreseeing the consequences that were going to result from it. Yet consequences had been evident in some areas as early as the reign of Francis II.

To this point the Protestants had not ceased to show their loyalty towards the representatives of the monarchy. When they were persecuted, they always invoked the sole justice of the lawful magistrate, and then appealed from it to the King, whom they held to be better informed. With the institution of protectors chosen within the nobility, without delegation from above and beyond the control of the sovereign authority, there developed among the Protestants the habit of having recourse to a power that stood apart from, if it was not actually hostile to, official jurisdiction.

It would be wrong to assume that the respect and affection of subjects for the person of the King were necessarily diminished, but in the minds of simple people the authority and prestige of titular officers and local functionaries were gravely impaired. It became easy to have the opinion popularly accepted that the true interpreters of the royal will were not the representatives of the administration but the nobles, the "protectors." This opinion was even more acceptable when, after the death of Henry II, the pamphleteers of Condé unceasingly maintained the argument that the sovereign was the prisoner of his ministers. In this way the communities gradually surrendered their fate to the will of the nobility. The "protector" became the patron and the patron became the master.

Even within the churches the situation seemed bound to work against religious authority and in favour of the group who controlled material force. The practical and fully-experienced tutelage of the nobility increasingly limited the spiritual and moral influence of the pastors on their flock. Direction of the movement escaped, in fact, from the control of Geneva, which became merely a theological centre and a seminary. It was Condé and no longer Calvin who gave the orders.

The Genevan reformers, who were disturbed by the actions of the nobles, and yet were usually powerless to avert their effects, struggled unceasingly against this situation throughout the years 1560 and 1561. The struggle was a moving one, in which the royal power, by persecuting the churches, favoured its most bitter enemies, the feudatories. The publicists of the reign of Francis II, who were so favourably inclined towards the Bourbons and so sparing of detail about the profound distortion of the Huguenot party, let slip several significant admissions which underlined the complaints and remonstrances of Calvin. They spoke of the intervention within the communities of

> several young noblemen, some attracted by novelties and with little understanding, others moved by a zeal which, nevertheless, had need of being tempered by discretion.

They pointed to the influence of

> newcomers and over-bold undertakers [*entrepreneurs*] who do not wish to subject themselves to the established consistory and distrust those who have laid the foundations of their church.

These were the men, these noble "undertakers" who, despite the preachers, had already urged the people to attack the convents and the Catholic churches at Valence, Romans and Montélimar, and who were later going to recruit the guerrilla bands of Baron des Adrets. There were the men who from 1560 "militarized" the ardent Provençal communities under the orders of de Mouvans and de Montbrun, "touring the churches to find out the number of their fighting men," raising captains, soldiers and volunteers, and then traversing the country breaking "images," until a pitiless repression set in for people of humble estate. Not just in a few regions, but throughout France, the material arm of the Reformation developed in 1561 to the detriment of spiritual influences, and in 1562 many ministers were actually reduced to the role of chaplains to the seigneurs.

And yet it should not be concluded that the responsibility and the initiative in all the acts of violence committed by the Huguenots should be attributed to the nobles. Purely popular riots occurred, especially in the towns. But, before 1562 at least, instances of demagogy were generally limited to certain regions where misery was extreme. In the spring of that year there was a general explosion of a revolutionary nature that marked the beginning of the civil war.

The movement by which the dissident nobility superimposed a military system on the religious organisation of the churches constitutes one of the cardinal facts of the period 1560–1562. It would be necessary to follow closely the smallest events in the local life of each province to grasp its full importance. In so doing one would certainly discover immediate chains of cause and effect which escape us here. In any case it is certain that this movement was aided by the increased domination of the laity in the synods.

The "protectors" offered the communities a help they needed, and they bestowed on French Protestantism the appearance of a material power. But they paralysed the moral force of Protestant propaganda. The entry of the nobility into the churches was to excite the fatal distrust of those middle classes wherein Calvin's doctrine had found its best-prepared and most-educated disciples. Now, the nobility could only furnish the churches with recruits who were relatively few in number, and who, in the profound task of spreading the gospel, were assuredly inferior to their bourgeois counterparts.

Political Anarchy and Social Discontent

HENRI HAUSER

Henri Hauser (1866–1946) held an honorary professorship in the Faculty of Letters in the University of Paris in the later years of his distinguished career. Although his special interests lay in the economic history of sixteenth-century France, his first book was a biography of the Huguenot paladin, François de la Noue (1892). He is remembered also for his four-volume analysis of the sources of French history in the period. Economic and social preoccupations are evident in his studies of the Reformation. His general view of the price revolution in the sixteenth century is best known to English-speaking students through his survey of early modern French economic history published in *Economic Review* in 1933 (it appeared in *Revue historique* in the following year). Here he claims that before the Wars of Religion the inflationary influences of American bullion stimulated a wave of commercial prosperity and proto-capitalism, although it depressed the real value of the incomes of the landed nobility living on fixed rents, and also produced distress among urban artisans. These interpretations have since been criticized, and his volume devoted to the history of prices from 1500 to 1800 has been largely superseded. He repeated his views, however, in his study of the economic policies of Cardinal Richelieu, published shortly before the author's death. The following extract is taken from Hauser's general history of the period, a work of brilliant synthesis.

THE DEATH of Henry II posed a series of redoubtable problems in France. The King was killed by a splinter of wood entering his eye, and rarely have such momentous consequences appeared to follow from so slight an instrument. The work of the three preceding kings, even that of Louis XI, was placed in jeopardy. It seemed as though a number of trends had been arrested and relegated to the past. Such trends were the transformation of the monarchy from a feudal to an administrative institution, the virtual completion of the process of centralisation, the extension of French influence throughout the then-known world, and the pursuit of what in several senses amounted to a policy of French expansion, holding in check the threatening might of the Burgundian-Hapsburg empire. It was far from clear that the peace of 1559 had already given a new direction to French history. The events of 1560–1562 both precipitated and clarified this change of course.

It is true that Francis II, the fifteen-year-old king, was past the age of minority, but he was ailing and appeared marked for early death, full of cholic and nervous disorders, and given to exhausting himself in exercise beyond his strength. He had three brothers, Charles, Alexandre (later to be called Henry), and Hercule (who was to be known as Francis), and three sisters, all of them in greater or less degree suffering the defects of the unhealthy stock of the Valois and Medici. As she was later to write after the death of Francis II, their mother was already dismayed to find herself "left with three (or four at that time) young boys, and a kingdom completely divided within itself, and not a single person to whom I could turn with any confidence." The young king was under the thumb of his seventeen-year-old wife, Mary Stuart, titular Queen of Scotland, clever,

From Henri Hauser, *La Préponderance espagnole,* Vol. IX of *Peuples et Civilisations* (Paris, 1948), pp. 42–46, 60. Reprinted by permission of Presses Universitaires de France. [Editor's translation.]

charming, but also in ill-health. Mary Stuart had her close relatives, the family of Guise, a younger branch of the house of Lorraine: the Cardinal, described by the Tuscan ambassador as both "Pope and King" in France, and the Duke of Guise, the conqueror of Calais. Both scorned the "Florentine merchant," though at first they were her allies; they served her spite and, at the same time, their own ambitions by exiling the late king's favourites, Diane de Poitiers and the Constable Montmorency. They also humiliated the Bourbons, and regarded themselves as the masters of France.

Henry II had left them with a tangled financial situation, and it must be admitted that they faced difficulties with great energy. They paid off the armed forces, suppressed pensions and revoked past alienations of the royal domain. Such a policy drew down upon them the hatred of a large section of the nobility, who were already ruined by the diminution of their feudal revenues. This hungry band of country squires laid siege to the court, and followed it threateningly from place to place while claiming the money to which their services entitled them.

The memory of the treason of the Constable of Bourbon against Francis I had long lain heavily upon the Bourbon family. Nevertheless, their title of "Princes of the Blood" allowed them to oppose the Lorrainers and to represent a kind of aristocratic nationalism in contrast to the "foreign princes." There were three Bourbon princes: Antoine de Vendôme, whose marriage with the daughter of Henri d'Albret and the sister of Francis I had brought him the title of King of Navarre, Louis de Condé and the Cardinal Charles, in addition to their relatives, the Montpensiers. In opposition to the Guises they drew close to the old Constable Montmorency, living in disgrace. But around the latter — faithful Catholic as he was — were gathered his three nephews, the Chastillons. They were particularly brilliant examples of the type of seigneurial nobility who shared the great offices of church and state: Odet, the Cardinal-Bishop of Beauvais; Gaspard de Coligny, Admiral of France, the defender of Saint-Quentin; François d'Andelot who succeeded to his brother's title of Colonel-General of the Infantry. All these possessed a subtle maturity of outlook, and because of their more or less open support for Protestantism they were regarded with suspicion by some and eagerly sought after by others. The Montmorencys and Chastillons were followed by a numerous clientèle.

In the death of the King who had persecuted them, the Protestants had seen the arm of divine justice. But Philip II offered to put troops at his nephew's disposal to exterminate heresy. The Guises agreed with the old Cardinal de Tournon that the persecution should become more pitiless than ever. Du Bourg, a judge at the court of the parlement was burned in the last days of 1559, while royal edicts and the declarations of the parlement reinforced the edict of Ecouen, and a campaign of terror reigned in Paris.

However, it was already too late to suppress heresy. The map of French Protestantism about 1560, in so far as it can be adequately sketched, is a striking one. The suburb of Saint-Germain was "a little Geneva." Meaux remained a centre of ardent faith. In Normandy towns such as Dieppe, Rouen, Caen, Saint-Lô could count their Protestants by thousands, including lawyers, merchants, clergy, royal officials, sailors and artisans. Brittany was touched by heresy and d'Andelot dominated the area around Nantes. Orléans, which occupied a strategic position of great importance, and acted as the point of contact for the Huguenot nobility of Anjou, Touraine and Berry, bore the appearance of a minor Huguenot capital. Metz was a Calvinist citadel. Although Champagne and Burgundy were still strongly under the influence of the Guises, conventicles continued to multiply there. Lyon, the great city of the fairs, quite close to Geneva, and the centre of the printers and weavers, was especially "infected," despite the efforts of Cardinal de Tournon and Saint-André, the Governor. From Lyons the new ideas descended the valley of the Rhône to Provence and laid siege to Auvergne and Vivarais. It was not just a question of the great consular towns, such as Nîmes and Montpellier, passing over to the Protestant side, but also of the majority of the small towns and country districts as far as the Cevennes and including Rouergue and the county of Foix. Turbulent Toulouse with its tumultuous university was sternly controlled by Montmorency. But the whole south-west was tainted with heresy. Memories of the revolts against the salt tax at Bordeaux, in Guyenne, Aunis and Saintonge, together with the influence of the little kingdom of Navarre and the court of Nérac, as well as the role of the merchant republic of La Rochelle and the neighbouring islands, favoured the spread of Protestant preaching and the increase of Protestant churches.

Though a precise figure cannot be given, it seems that in 1560 French Protestantism was a strong numerical force as well as a moral one. In 1561 Coligny spoke openly of 2500 "organised" churches, and a little later it was declared that 6000 ministers would have to be sent from Geneva before the needs of the new congregations could be satisfied. Persecution, far from stifling heresy, performed the role of publicising it. Poverty caused by the economic crisis favoured Protestantism, especially among the artisans. From 1558 Bernard Palissy shows us how on Sundays the journeymen of Saintes walked out into the country in groups singing psalms. In Limousin the pastors at first preached in the woods, but the bourgeoisie of Limoges accepted conversion, and all round the town there occurred "assemblies, sermons and baptisms and other sacraments according to the Genevan custom." Master craftsmen, journeymen and merchants were to be found on the lists of emigrants to Geneva and Lausanne, where the persecution had driven numbers of those classes that had no fixed roots. When the storm had passed the fugitives often returned to their home towns to spread the gospel there.

The one new element towards 1560 was the formation of a manorial Protestantism of seigneurs within the class of landed gentry of middling or small estate, whose discontents we have already mentioned. Philip II's ambassador, Chantonnay, reported to his master on 1st January 1560 that there were more than 2000 of them. Like Jeanne d'Albret in her Pyrenean kingdom, or the consuls in their towns, these rude country gentry unconsciously put into practice the doctrine of *cujus regio hujus religio* (a man's religion must be that of the ruler of his territory) and made many conversions of their vassals and those who paid them dues. "God," wrote one of them in 1561, "has given me authority to rule many men, and by my agency one of the most superstitious districts in the kingdom may be gained for Christ." In rural Protestantism, which was generally less in strength than the Protestantism of the towns, the petty Protestant gentry occupied positions of increasing importance, and the châtelain became the natural protector of those churches constituted within his lands. Suddenly the French Protestant movement experienced a change of direction. In the words of the metaphor used by the pastors, a hammer was fashioned instead of an anvil. The new leaders of the movement were not men whose humour would allow them to suffer the treatment accorded the wool carders of Meaux or the "poor unlettered artisans" of Guyenne. These were men such as Montgomery, whose involuntary slaying of Henry II in the lists caused Catherine de Medici to have him pursued as a murderer; as the family of Rohan-Soubise in the west; as the multitude of petty seigneurs from Dauphiné, Gascony, and Provence; as the lesser Breton nobility, won over by d'Andelot, who had had necessarily to be freed from imprisonment — not to speak of such a prince of the blood as Condé. The era of persecution was to be followed by that of resistance, and soon by that of revolt. Elements of social and political discontent were to become much more significant than religious faith in the complex attitudes of the new Protestants, and thenceforth it became possible to speak of "political" as well as of "religious" Huguenots.

. . . Thus in France under the last Valois kings there began an era of civil wars lasting about thirty years. Much skill has been applied by historians to enumerating the various phases and naming them the first, second, third, etc. of the Wars of Religion. In reality these conflicts absorbed the energies of a turbulent and warlike nobility which had previously been expressed in foreign campaigns. The wars were also the revolts of towns or of provinces resentful of the centralisation pursued by the monarchy. They were in part promoted by the intrigues of foreign powers, desiring sometimes to support one of the contending parties and sometimes even to profit from the weakness of the royal authority and carve off for themselves some slice of French territory. They were wars interrupted less by true peace treaties than by periods of truce, during which the ties of family, neighbourhood and friendship were renewed between enemies, who yesterday had been cutting each other's throats and tomorrow would be setting about the same business. They were wars of atrocity, where the two parties emulated each other in their unspeakable cruelties, massacres of Protestants, hangings of priests, mass executions and savage tortures, the breaking of statues, the profanation and destruction of churches, and the pillage of sacred things. They were wars where set battles were complicated by small local struggles between town and town, château and château.

The Failure of Catherine de Medici

SIR JOHN NEALE

Sir John Neale, the doyen of Elizabethan scholars, was born in 1890. He was appointed assistant in History at University College, London, under the direction of A. F. Pollard, the Tudor historian, in 1919. He was Professor of History at Manchester University for three years and in 1928 assumed the Astor Chair of English History at University College, where he remained until he retired and became Professor Emeritus in 1956. His best known books are his biography of Queen Elizabeth and his accounts of her parliaments. His short survey of the French Wars of Religion was written to complement his Elizabethan studies. His strictures on Catherine de Medici, when compared with the English Queen, are often severe. The following passage discusses the origins of the civil wars in terms of the financial crisis at the death of Henry II, and the inability of the Queen Mother to solve the political and religious problems confronting her when she became regent eighteen months later.

EARLIER in the narrative I said that modern research has a very up-to-date reason for the making of the Peace of Cateau-Cambrésis: money. We may take this as the starting point for examining the condition in which the long period of the Italian Wars, and their last phase in particular, had left France. For some time —

From Sir John Neale, *The Age of Catherine de Medici* (London: Jonathan Cape Ltd., 1943; New York: Barnes and Noble, Inc., 1959), pp. 33–42, 52–58. Reprinted by permission of Jonathan Cape Ltd.

in fact, since the reign of that extravagant and picturesque king, Francis I — war had become ruinously expensive. Henry VIII of England had discovered this in the latter years of his reign, and, although he had the wealth of the monasteries on which to fall back, his by-no-means spectacular military adventures undermined English government finance. It was the misfortune of Europe, and especially of Spain and France, that the disastrous business of war, with its new and costly methods, could go on because international business and credit were just developing on a modern scale and could be made the means by which kings might impoverish their own and other countries. As yet the evil of credit inflation had not been realized, and bankers and others were therefore the easy victims of a royal rake's progress.

Now it so happens — and this is significant for our study of the Age of Catherine de Medici — that the first great credit inflation of modern times, with its nemesis of state bankruptcy, took place in the years 1557 and 1558, setting in motion a series of financial crises that were to last through the rest of the century and on into the next. This inflation was the result of the last phases of the war between France and Spain. Both countries had needed very large sums of money — far beyond their immediate or, with safety, their prospective revenues — to carry on the war. And both countries had developed the instrument of credit. They had established what we term funded debts — permanent state loans, the interest on which formed annuities for those investing in them. The French call these *rentes,* and quite small people had their savings invested in them in the sixteenth century as to-day. The *rentier* class in France had been in existence and had been growing since the 1520's.

However, the main monetary resources for war came, not from permanent but from short-term loans, raised by the French king mainly at the great banking centre of Lyons, and by the Spanish king at Antwerp. At first these loans had been regarded by individual bankers with suspicion, but the habit of making them grew, and as the interest that kings were ready to pay increased to twelve per cent and then sixteen per cent, the prospect of a fine bargain broke down restraint. In 1555 Henry II of France carried through a transaction, the name of which we may translate as the Great Deal. He renewed his immense loans at Lyons, some of which had been at twelve per cent interest, contracted new loans, and put both old and new on a sixteen per cent interest basis. The transaction created a kind of South Sea Bubble. Everyone rushed to share in the Deal, layman and professional, widow and merchant, prince and gentleman, French, Swiss, German, even the Turk.

At the same time Philip II of Spain was working the money market at Antwerp for all that he was worth, or rather, for a great deal more. Both kings had outrun their resources, though their war needs were by no means satisfied. Nemesis followed. In 1557 Philip went bankrupt. Henry II managed to fool his creditors for a few months by asserting that the King of France would not break his word; and oddly enough there were people ready to believe him. Then he too defaulted. The credit inflation burst; and to put it rather crudely both kings had to make peace because wars then as now were fought on paper — paper-credit — and supplies had disappeared.

Financial stability is of course one of the main sources of the strength of a state; and here was the French State about to enter a critical period in its history with its credit ruined and colossal debts. The debt at the death of Henry II was over forty million *livres;* the royal income then, much of which never reached the Treasury, was approximately twelve million. The *livre* equalled about two shillings of contemporary English money, and perhaps some idea of the meaning of these sums may be obtained by remembering that Queen Elizabeth's annual revenue at the beginning of her reign averaged little more than a quarter of a million pounds.

A desperate budgetary position was not the only lamentable consequence of the war period. Naturally enough, the French monarchy had exploited taxation as well as other devices for raising revenue, to their extreme limits; and these limits, it is worth noting, were much greater than in England, where direct taxation could only be levied through parliament. The French king could tax on his own authority. So heavy, in fact, did the main direct tax — the *taille* — become that peasants left their lands and fled from it. There were certain sections of the country, of which Normandy was an example, where for various reasons the exactions and abuses of the government could go further than elsewhere; and these provinces readily lent themselves to Huguenot propaganda. Generally speaking, social discontent found an outlet for itself in religious and political unrest.

The machinery of government itself suffered from the financial straits of the monarchy. French local government was already very different from that in England which remained in the unpaid hands of the landed gentry; and while the rapid increase of governmental activity associated with the rise of the modern state was accompanied by a remarkable expansion of the administrative duties of the English gentry as Justices of the Peace, in France the nobility or landed gentry were stripped of their feudal share in the government of the country, and more and more the business of local government, like that of central government, was placed in the hands of lawyer-officials of the State. This growing bureaucracy ought to have been a source of strength to the French monarchy, to which the professional administrator owed office, salary, and career. But in its overwhelming need for money, the Crown had taken a page out of the Papacy's book and had recourse to the sale of offices: officials were compelled to purchase their posts. Control was inevitably sacrificed, for a bureaucracy cannot be disciplined without the right of dismissal, and this had virtually gone. Thus when the severe trial of civil war fell on the French monarchy, one of the chief means of governing was deficient.

The mere sale of offices was not all; for Henry II, again like the Papacy, had taken to the creation of new offices and the multiplication of old, not because the administration required an increase of officials, but because the Crown needed ready money for new wars and could obtain it in this way. The policy was hopelessly short-sighted. Salaries were small, yet were often not paid. In 1559 the whole royal pay-roll, from high officials to common soldiers, was badly in arrears, in many instances for years. Officials had to recoup themselves from the wretched people who came under their charge or needed to use their services. And thus to the crippling burden of taxation was added the vexatious weight of official exactions.

Another element of weakness was the state of the lesser nobility or country gentlemen. As a class they were vulnerable at two points where the English gentry were protected. In the first place, the system of entail of estates, with descent to the eldest son only — a system which, whatever its injustice, has the advantage of preserving the wealth and standing of a family through generations — was not rigorously applied. Estates were constantly being broken up and the wealth of the main line of a noble house diminished. Secondly, in the sixteenth century a final ban was placed on the entry of French noblemen and their children into trade. In contrast with the custom of England, all the sons of the nobility were noble. They were thus precluded from that salutary participation in commerce which refreshed the wealth of the English gentry. For the younger sons of the gentry, cursed with the empty dignity of nobility, war was the only career; and as that career was closed by the termination of the Italian Wars in 1559 they were left without employment. And to make matters worse, they had latterly been fighting without pay since the royal Treasury was empty.

The lesser nobility in 1559 were in a

very bad way. Their social functions had largely gone with the transfer of local government from them to lawyer-bureaucrats. They were immune in theory from the main tax, the *taille;* but in practice this was not entirely true, and in any case they had to bear an appreciable part of the financial burden. They had been compelled to contribute to forced loans; they had been victims of the great speculation in royal loans at luring but unpaid interest; in 1555 they had been cruelly hit by a heavy royal levy of money. And they found themselves in a ruinous age. Their rank compelled them to spend money on the education of their children and burdened them with the growing luxury in dress and display, while the great price-revolution in the second half of the sixteenth century, which caused a slump in the value of money at least as drastic as that in our own lifetime since 1914, played havoc with their finances, since rentals tended to remain fixed. Last blow of all, peace brought an end to their career of war.

They raised mortgages, they went bankrupt. And as in England in the sixteenth century, though to a far greater extent, they saw merchants and the lawyer-sons of merchants ousting them from their estates, becoming country gentry, and receiving patents of nobility. Some noblemen in desperation took to brigandage, forming those bands of marauders who were recruited for the Conspiracy of Amboise and were later to help in making the Religious Wars scenes of murder and rapine.

The picture which I have drawn is that of a country needing above all things a period of peace, firm government and retrenchment. This was not to be. In June 1559, during a tilt at celebrations connected with the Peace of Cateau-Cambrésis the King, Henry II, whose folly and prodigality had brought France to the verge of ruin, was mortally wounded. He left a family of four boys, the eldest of whom and the successor to the throne, Francis II, was only fifteen.

In the New Monarchies of the sixteenth century, government was essentially personal. Its whole mechanism, from the core of councillors whom the King chose to advise him, reflected the personality of the monarch. Loyalty was a personal feeling towards the King, not towards the abstraction of the State; and the secret of successful government was that power should rest on this loyalty and both be merged in the Crown. Obviously a boy could be no more than the titular repository of power. The reality must be somewhere else. Consequently, power was bound to become an object of competition among the various claimants to it at Court.

England under Edward VI demonstrated this sixteenth-century truth; and the rivalry of the great lords, Somerset and Northumberland, for the control of power is one of the notorious passages of our history. Who, then, were the Somersets and Northumberlands of France? Who were the leading personalities at Court and what Court parties were there at this time?

The answer must begin with the Queen-Mother, Catherine de Medici. She was just forty years old at the death of her husband, Henry II. She was a daughter of the Medici, the ruling House of Florence, and niece of the Medici Pope Clement VII. Her marriage at the age of fourteen and a half to Henry, then only the second son of Francis I and unlikely to succeed to the throne, had been a move in Francis I's Italian diplomacy. It was a *mésalliance:* indeed, how else could the marriage of a French king's son to the daughter of an Italian merchant family — for that was the origin of the Medici — be regarded? But it was to be justified by Papal policy. Unfortunately Pope Clement died in less than a year, and the justification did not mature. Then, the death of the Dauphin made Henry the heir to the throne, thus aggravating the blunder of the marriage; and, final catastrophe, for seven years Catherine remained childless. For a time there was talk of repudiating her, and, no doubt, if she had continued childless we should have had a "divorce" that might have helped to make the marital adventures of Henry VIII of England a little more understandable to modern writers. The situation called for all Catherine's skill and sweetness to postpone a decision. Children alone could save her. And at last they came. In rapid succession she bore ten. The danger was past.

. . . A fairly stern school of experience: life had certainly been that for Catherine. She never overcame the sense of her inferior origin, and her exaggerated respect for royalty was time and again to influence her policy. She pursued crowns for her children as wealthy American matrons — according to repute — once pursued titled husbands for their daughters. She was not an intellectual, nor was she genuinely cultured, but as a true daughter of the Italian Renaissance she liked to patronize the arts and have the trappings of culture about her. She had a live sense of the splendour of royalty, derived from the extravagant Court of her father-in-law, Francis I, and, being a very rich woman in her private fortune, she indulged her taste for showiness and was insatiate in her love of building. Her reckless extravagance in the midst of the terrible financial distress of her country is not a pleasing aspect of her character.

She was undoubtedly a woman of great qualities, if not a great woman. Her vitality was boundless: she was always ready, with tireless energy, to tackle every difficulty that arose. But she lacked any grasp of principles, and was apt to see political problems in terms of a Palace intrigue which could be solved by getting folk together and making them shake hands. She was, in fact, a politician, a very able politician, not a statesman; and her charm coupled with her vitality made her most successful at the game.

Modern psychologists would shake their heads over her possessive maternalism. She loved her children and dominated them with her affection and personality in a way that was ruinous to them. The blackest event in her whole story — the Massacre of St. Bartholomew — had its roots in this instinct. To a certain extent it was her desire to mother her children that led her to desire the regency of France, though once she had tasted political power her energy led her to guard and monopolize it with passion.

* * *

. . . [After the death of Francis II in December 1560] appeasement was now the ruling idea, and the year that followed was to see this policy put to its crucial tests. Peace depended on the solution of two problems: Court faction, and religion. Catherine's solution for the first was to keep both Bourbons and Guise at Court, behaving like bosom friends. When their real feelings betrayed themselves in squabbles, she hurried to make them friends again, as one might try to keep two naughty quarrelsome boys in order by love and sweets. It was a nice, motherly policy; but it was not statesmanship, and we shall later see its fatal error.

Catherine's solution for the religious problem, while bound to command respect in the more tolerant atmosphere of later centuries, was no more statesmanlike in its own *milieu* than her handling of the political problem. She contemplated a temporary policy leading to a permanent solution. Temporarily, she determined to continue that partial toleration of Huguenots which had been inaugurated on her initiative during the troubles at Amboise. With this in view she issued a new amnesty, releasing religious prisoners, even those imprisoned for causing disturbances; and at the same time she urged officials to exercise a toleration beyond the terms of her edict. The practical consequence, of course, was to encourage the growth of the Huguenot movement, increase the bitterness of religious feeling everywhere, and make the religious problem graver than ever. The Easter of 1561 was a time of great disorder throughout the land.

It would be a signal error to imagine that Catherine meant either to recognize the Huguenot faith or permanently to tolerate two faiths. Both Calvinists and Catholics would have regarded the latter as sacrilege, and to politicians of that epoch it would have been an assault on national unity. Toleration, as that age saw it, was not homage to the rights of conscience, but the recognition that one of two faiths was not strong enough to suppress the other, or that it would only succeed in doing so at the cost of wrecking the State.

If, then toleration was merely a temporary policy, what was Catherine's permanent solution for the religious problem? It was a National Council of the French Church with a programme of reform, doctrinal and disciplinary, that would unite Catholic and Protestant.

For some years sovereigns had been urging the Papacy to summon a Council of the whole Church. Such a Council had sat twice at Trent, the last time in 1551–52, when it had adjourned to another meeting. Now this Council had come to decisions that made a compromise between Catholicism and Protestantism, desired by an influential section of Christendom, impossible. Consequently, in demanding another Council those who still hoped for compromise were emphatic that the Council of Trent must be allowed to lapse and an entirely new one be summoned, not bound by its decisions. The Papacy gave no signs of action; and Catherine de Medici and the Cardinal of Lorraine, who in this matter was for compromise with Protestantism and a broad Church settlement, hit upon the plan of calling a National Council of the Gallican Church. They hoped to arrange a compromise with Protestantism, and thus be ready with a *fait accompli* when the Oecumenical Council of the whole Church was at length summoned. The condition of the French Church, they argued, could not wait on Papal dilatoriness.

From the Papal point of view the policy was not wholly unacceptable but also extremely dangerous. It might lead to schism; and the notorious independence of the Gallican Church made a breach between France and Rome seem far from impossible. The Papacy met the danger by issuing a Bull announcing the continuation of the old Council of Trent, at the same time using all the vigour and threats of which it was capable to prevent the meeting of a French Council.

What was to be done? Catherine could not hold a National Council when an Oecumenical Council was summoned. On the other hand, to acquiesce in the re-summoning of the Council of Trent was to renounce all hope of settling the religious problem in France. She resolved the dilemma by dropping the name of Council from her assembly, disguising her intentions under the term "Colloquy"; and she proceeded with her plans in secret to avoid a direct Papal veto. Her Colloquy — the Colloquy of Poissy as it was called — was launched on an assembly of the French Church which met at the end of July 1561.

Catherine was playing with fire: there can be no doubt about it. And the Cardinal of Lorraine, who is credited by his latest biographer with responsibility for the scheme of a National Council, revealed, one may admit, a well-meaning tolerance but hardly great foresight or astute statesmanship. In order to arrange the representation of the Huguenot Church at the Colloquy, Catherine naturally turned to the Admiral Coligny, whose charm of manner and unselfish loyalty to the monarchy pleased her. She kept him at Court for advice, agreed to his suggestion that Calvin's right-hand man, Theodore Beza, should be brought from Geneva for the Colloquy, and herself suggested Peter Martyr of Zurich. She actually received these notorious heretics at Court; and inevitably the Huguenots in Court circles, with such leaders present and in high favour, flaunted their faith and worship as never before. Nor could or did all this happen without encouraging the Huguenot movement everywhere.

Catherine's policy could only be justified if it had an appreciable chance of success. In fact it had none. Neither the Catholic Church nor the Calvinist was purely national. Each was controlled from a headquarters over which the French King had no control; and force or cajolery was incapable of imposing a settlement on Rome or

Geneva. The truth is that Catherine was blind to the difficulties that she was up against. Her Colloquy would necessarily handle doctrinal problems; but, as a contemporary said, she herself had no idea what the word "dogma" meant.

The assembly opened. Catherine succeeded in her trick of turning it into a Colloquy. And then the trouble started. Orthodox Catholics cried out in horror at a figure of speech used by Beza. She smoothed this out. Then, when further difficulties arose, she tried to overcome them by gathering the leading Catholic and Protestant divines together in private. She was under the illusion that differences over the Eucharist could be solved as she had been solving the quarrels of Bourbon and Guise in the last nine months — by bringing the quarrelsome people together and persuading them to be friendly. She meant well; she laboured hard; she failed. Fundamental differences of principle are not to be resolved by mediators who have no principles.

Catherine's policy was a catastrophe. On the one hand, by seeming to give recognition to their faith she had bred in Huguenot ranks a new spirit of daring that displayed itself in the wholesale seizing of churches. On the other hand, she had enraged the Catholics, who turned on the Huguenots and massacred them. But in spite of all this, Catherine persisted in her policy of seeking for a peaceful settlement. She kept Beza and Coligny at Court to pacify the Huguenots and check excesses by their influence. What wonder if this merely added to the demoralization, apparently confirming the impression that the Court supported the Huguenots? So thoroughly did she play her game that Beza himself thought that he was about to convert the King and the Queen-Mother to Calvinism!

The extent of the catastrophe has been only half told. In tackling the problem of political faction, Catherine had concentrated all her attention on maintaining friendship between Bourbon and Guise and keeping both parties at Court. Time and again she patched up their quarrels; but all the reconciliations were hollow and of short duration. Meanwhile, in constant pursuit of an elusive goal she had neglected the Montmorency, that vital centre group whose firm loyalty to the Crown made it the essential basis of a King's party. The way was thus free for Guise and the Constable Montmorency, dropping their long and traditional rivalry, to draw together. Both were now opposed to the Bourbons; both felt their Catholic faith threatened by the Queen-Mother's policy.

The result of this tragic neglect was seen when in April 1561, the Constable Montmorency, the Duke of Guise, and another nobleman formed what was known as the Triumvirate — a Catholic party or league. It marks a turning point in our story. For now a party existed, menacing in its power, whose object was to defend the Catholic faith, apart from the King and if need be against him.

The Crown was thus isolated between two parties of passion — Catholic and Huguenot — with all the Court factions on one side or the other. It was unable to control events or prevent the outbreak of civil war: indeed, by flirting with heresy and so fanning the flames of religious strife, Catherine de Medici had unwittingly hastened the day when the calamity of civil war would fall on France.

II. CHARACTER

Protestant Democratic Liberty and Sinister Catholic Conspiracy

JULES MICHELET

Jules Michelet (1798–1874) was the most celebrated of nineteenth-century romantic historians, and his colourful and highly subjective work still exerts an influence in French public opinion, if not in academic circles. Despite the poverty of his boyhood he had a brilliant academic career and became Professor of Ancient History at the *Ecole normale supérieure* at the age of twenty-eight. He was subsequently custodian of the National Archives, where he prepared the early volumes of his history of France. He interrupted this history in 1843, five years after his appointment to the Chair of History at the Collège de France, to write his fervent and imaginative study of the French Revolution. He lost his posts in 1851 through his refusal to support the Second Empire, and returned to his general history. The extract that follows belongs to this portion of the work, which began to be issued in 1855 with the declaration in the preface that it was "written not to trouble those elements from the past that are dying but to appeal to those that are vital and alive." Michelet's romantic vision schematized history in terms of revolutionary liberty and popular democracy. His persuasive eloquence has made his work a historical force in itself.

By 1558] it was time, time indeed, for Protestantism to take up the sword and look to its defence. It would certainly have perished if it had not become an armed party. Significant events — events a hundred times more important than the futile war between the two Catholic courts of Hapsburg and Valois — had taken place in the religious sphere. The supreme question of the age stood revealed. It had been disclosed in England under the bloody terror of Mary Tudor. In France it burnt like some subterranean fire, casting a jet of flame from the darkness. Before these portents the Kings were ready to come to terms, to end a conflict devoid of meaning, to declare that they agreed in designating Protestant freedom as their sole enemy, and to turn their strength against it.

In the Low Countries, in England, in Italy, in Spain and in France, in both north and south, everything was concerted to stifle Protestantism. The French Reformation could say to its children, as the wolf in the fable said to its cubs: "Climb to the top of the mountain and look towards the four winds: as far as you can see you will behold no one save your enemies."

Germany was no friend. Through their success over Charles V the Lutherans had become an officially recognised party, an established church. They were now secure within the political framework of the Empire, and much less disposed to abandon

From Jules Michelet, *Histoire de France* (1.III *Guerres de Religion,* 1.IV *La Ligue et Henri IV*), 3 vols., édition Rouff (Paris, N.D.) vol. 2, pp. 1138–1340, 1348–1350, 1399–1400, 1508–1511. [Editor's translation.]

their security and risk the adventure of new wars to support Calvinism in contradiction of the Lutheran interest. They were Germans as well as Lutherans, and they hated France for the theft of the three bishoprics [Metz, Toul and Verdun]. French Protestants were none the less Frenchmen as far as they were concerned. Nor could the French Reformation hope for greater help from the Catholic or Protestant Swiss — especially when the Swiss were in the pay of the French and Spanish monarchies.

The Christian answer in such a predicament was doubtless to accept martyrdom, to offer one's neck to the executioner and to expect to triumph through suffering. The philosophers and self-appointed guardians of civilisation would presumably have advised waiting for events to take their course, trusting the all-powerful light of new-born liberty to win through in the end. But these were answers that suited tyrants: indeed they were just what tyrants demanded. Martyrdom had been accepted unresistingly for the preceding forty years. As Christians, pacifically-minded townsmen, workers or merchants, had surrendered themselves for butchery. What was more, they had seen their wives and children burned without a word of protest. This excessive, one might say unnatural, submission to the powers that represented the flails of God was a betrayal of the family. The innocent souls of the weak, whose protection should have been a sacred duty, were delivered up not only to death but to temptation, corruption and damnation. Some might insist that primitive Christianity had triumphed by patience and the stubbornness of its martyrs; but there were other considerations, such as the strength that came from a great social revolution within the lower classes, from conquest and the sword of Constantine.

So much for the Christians. It may also be asked what would have become of the Renaissance, since the men of the Renaissance had yielded to a tranquil inertia which obscured their vision. The light of the Renaissance, instead of growing in intensity, was going out. A vast extension of the conspiracy of Catholic piety, coupled with the materialism of Ignatius Loyola, was taking place. On the other hand, fools were replacing the bearers of light: Ronsard was eclipsing Rabelais. The sceptical, individualist, pessimistic book of Montaigne represented a great decline from the lively optimism of the work of Rabelais. Natural science, which had shone so brilliantly at the beginning of the century, had become weak and enfeebled. The heroes of science had served as martyrs. Paracelsus, the Luther of science, had been killed. So, too, had perished Vesalius, the doctor of Charles V and the Christopher Columbus of anatomy — or, at least, he had died of hunger on a desert island. Goujon, Ramus and Goudimel had been killed in a single day. Such men were irreplaceable, and both history and common sense declare that creativity is not automatically engendered.

No, if the Protestants had not unsheathed the sword — if they had not become a great armed force which pursued the quest for liberty in England and the Netherlands beyond the boundaries of the condemned continent — if the conquering fleets of the Dutch had not kept safe one last refuge in Europe for human thought, then the new rays of light would never have been seen. There would have been no Shakespeare, no Bacon, no Harvey, no Descartes, no Rembrandt, no Galileo. Galileo deserves mention in this context, for it was the telescope made in Holland that opened the heavens to his gaze.

Before studying the great conflict in which Protestantism preserved human freedom, it is appropriate to visit the Louvre, and in reverential mood to inspect the picture of Ruysdaël and Backhuyen, saluting therein the sacred tricolour flag of that Republic of Holland, which defended the world against Philip II and Louis XIV. When the true faith has won the victory, and the temples to the God of intellect have been erected, those pictures should be hung there which express the infinite within the infinitesimal space of their canvas. Such were the portraits composed by Rembrandt in the haven provided by his country, especially the portraits of his old teacher, who could no longer read, but who sat with his thoughts before the fire, and fixed his eyes on a globe in which, like some great cosmographer, he measured the seas — that battlefield of victory and arena of liberty.

A hundred years of conflict had to pass before that victory was gained in the seventeenth century. The victory could not have been secured without war and the use of the sword. We need not quibble at the fact that Protestant initiative had to pass from those peaceful classes who had allowed themselves to be slaughtered to the only military class that then existed, the nobility. It is a well-known trick of the enemies of liberty to stop at this point, and to appeal to our egalitarian instincts by asking whether one can accept such aristocratic leaders as William the Silent and Coligny. They ought indeed to be accepted, for they inured the people to war, and in consequence the people were in their turn ennobled.

Coligny and his brother, both colonels general of the French Infantry, were the rough, austere instructors of our soldiery of former times. They turned us into a fighting nation of the calibre of the men who, in the aftermath of St. Bartholomew when their leaders were slain, could confidently start the war once more in France and the Netherlands, and oblige the Kings to come to terms. These noblemen of the sword, who were the first to form the advance guard of liberty, deserve to be known as men of the people. The historian ought to do for them what was done for a member of the Genoese nobility when, although his class was excluded from office, he performed services for the state. He was rewarded by being degraded from the nobility and advanced to plebeian rank. No one deserves this reward more than does Coligny, for it was Coligny who, after a particular treaty, asked the prince de Condé: "Your treaty protects the nobles, the châteaux and the seigneurs, but who will protect the people of the towns?"

The Reformation seemed tied in a tangled knot that could not be unravelled. Despite the doctrines and the doctors who defended them, it was necessary for Protestantism to become a powerful armed force and to take up the gage of battle. Calvin had not hesitated to call upon force to execute justice. He had established the jurisdiction of the Genevan republic by condemning to death those former leaders of the city who would have surrendered it to Catholic France. It became a cruel limitation of the concept of the public welfare when, in order to survive, Geneva had to inflict wounds upon itself. When the so-called Libertines perished they took with them their friend, the unfortunate Servet. The Italian and Spanish reformers at Geneva, whose rationalism sapped the unity of the Genevan community, were obliged to seek safety in flight. In England in 1555 Protestants were burned for making too much of the power of reason: in Geneva Calvin insisted that philosophers could not be Protestants.

Calvin did not contest the right of secular authority to punish. He acknowledged it as representing the power of God. Kings were divinely instituted and it was vain for private men to dispute as to what was the best form of government. If the subjects of princes used such an argument to justify revolt, "it would be foolish and evil speculation. Although those who possess the sword may be enemies of God, He has instituted kingdoms so that men may live in peace and without fear." Such was the doctrine of Geneva. If Geneva was the mainspring of the Protestant cause as a republican stronghold and a seminary for martyrs, it was also the source of its weakness, through its doctrine of authority and its respect for secular powers.

Salvation came, I believe, through two means — means by which the Protestant church unwittingly broke free from Genevan domination. Our French nobility, which had been ruined by the court and the shameful reign of Diane de Poitiers, had retained scant respect for an authority that had fallen into feminine hands. They acquired a love and admiration for men of austerity, whose way of life revealed the full measure of the disgrace of the monarchy. To the nobility the ideal of duty seemed incarnate in Coligny. Secondly, the example of the Scottish nobility (with their acceptance of the "covenants" devised by the agitator John Knox in a manner far more positive than Calvin's) modified French Protestantism at an early stage. It served as a counterweight to the system of passive obedience still maintained by the Genevan doctors.

* * *

If ever a blow was struck by the hand of God, the death of Henry II was such an instance of divine intervention. The Protestants assumed it to be so. Some unidentified Protestant even dared to place among the hangings in the room where the corpse was lying a tapestry showing St. Paul struck dumb on the road to Damascus as he heard the voice thunder from the skies: "Why do you persecute your God, oh Saul?"

An act which was equally daring in another way had just taken place secretly in Paris. Let us call it by its true name, of which even those who participated in it were ignorant: the Protestant Republic. From 26th to 29th May a general assembly of French pastors met in the suburb of Saint-Germain. During the violent debates in the Parlement, close by the execution pyres, and in the midst of a frenzied population who would even massacre Catholics suspected of toleration, these intrepid men came from every Province in France to sit in council. In their strength and high seriousness they inscribed their faith, their discipline and the foundation of religious democracy.

The impulse for this act came neither from Paris nor Geneva: it was principally the result of necessity. The French Reformation had undergone a vast underground expansion and consisted of a throng of churches, born from spontaneous inspiration or missionary activity in caverns, barns, woods and solitary moors. Great diversity existed. There were few links between the congregations and they differed without realising it, in organisation and discipline. Choudieu [la Roche Chandieu], a pastor in Paris, was sent by his church to the synod at Poitiers. He brought there, or, perhaps, found there, the idea of establishing an agreement between the churches of France. The place of meeting was to be Paris, in the fiery centre of the persecution. The suburb of Saint-Germain, which in those days was being built outside the city walls, offered some means of concealment for this secret assembly.

In discipline and in faith the intention was to return to the primitive church, as Geneva had endeavoured to do. "No church will be superior to others. The ministers will assemble twice a year, each bringing with him an elder and a deacon. A new minister *elected by the elders and deacons* is to be presented to the congregation for which he is ordained. If any oppose him, the matter will be judged in the consistory or the provincial synod, not in such a way as would constrain the people to receive the elected minister, but rather to justify his claims as a minister." This was the republican basis of the church of France. It was truly republican then, for *the electors* (elders and deacons) were first *themselves elected by the people.*

All this was copied from Geneva, but it proved very different in effect when the organisation suited to a small town was applied to the kingdom of France, and generally to that vast empire which the Reformation was in process of creating in the Netherlands, Scotland, England, and, soon, in America. The difference was yet more marked when the Protestant Republic was no longer limited to a town of refuge and instruction which was kept closed and defended, but had embarked upon a hazardous adventure in the great battlefields of civil war. It was doubtful whether the separate nature of the spiritual world in which the church hoped to preserve its identity could be seriously maintained. One could not be sure whether the words of the Gospel and the weapon of excommunication, which were the sole means of defence the church wished to possess, would be sufficient. The secular tyrants might not take such weapons very seriously. Would not the need to defend the people and the duty to protect the weak oblige the churches to take up some other sword? The issue was whether the Protestant Republic should become an armed republic. Scotland decided it must be so, but France at first refused to agree and still tried to follow the Genevan tradition and to remain loyal to the old spirit of Christian obedience.

* * *

[In June 1562] the Protestants throughout France paused momentarily when rumours of peace began to circulate. They were weakened and disconcerted, and when they measured the strength of their own resources they found them pitifully slight. It seemed that they were near to death. The nation was roused in opposition; the Parlement stirred up Paris against them. Sixty men had been killed at Vassy, but that, it seemed, mattered little. The hound of death (as the Catholics called the populace) had now been unleashed, and it remained only to observe it hunt its prey.

The year 1562 was as fearful a one as that in which the Massacre of St. Bartholomew occurred a decade later. The horrors of 1572 took place principally in Paris, whereas in 1562 the slaughter was general throughout France. Events in one town after another revealed three entirely new aspects. First, massacres inside the town walls; second, the maddened pursuit of the fugitives by the peasants; third (since so much blood did not slake these murderous appetites) the judges had yet to have their fill, and executions began on a vast scale. In one place three hundred persons were hanged: in another two hundred broken on the wheel.

Let us return for a moment to the month of April, when the news of the massacres at Vassy and Sens was still current. The Protestants had reacted violently, especially in the south, where the race was more passionate in temperament. There was never lack of pretext for murder along the Rhône, in the violent country of the Albigenses. Many priests were killed, but it must be said that for the most part vengeance was wreaked upon stones and images. The Protestant lower classes, often led by children at first, decapitated the images of the saints in the cathedrals. Celebrated relics that had performed many miracles were called on to achieve a new miracle to save themselves from destruction. These curers of universal ills, who had drawn men from such great distances, were powerless to cure themselves, and they were dragged down as liars, impostors, and charlatans. In this welter of destruction, there perished, along with the saints, several tombs of kings and princes. It was a foolish mob that broke dead idols and yet adored the living. It was absurd that a war for freedom should be waged *in the name of a prince of the blood* and *in the name of the King,* reputed to be the prisoner of the Guises.

As for those artistic monuments, whose loss I deplore as much as anyone, I am surprised that several authors, who pass lightly over the massacres, should shed such tears over stones. They call it irreparable disaster, but surely less irreparable than the loss of so many lives in the massacres. The cynical witticism of the mighty Condé surveying a battlefield, "Only a night's work in Paris," is false. The genius and virtues of the dead can never be replaced. That generation of slaughtered Protestants who had purified France, would, had they been spared, have saved the nation from the incredible moral collapse that followed—from the putrefaction of indifference and the hypocritical scepticism, whence liberty could scarce be resuscitated.

The good sense of the men of our day has been so distorted, and our associates have so readily swallowed the gross lies thrown to them by our enemies, that they believe and repeat the fables that the Protestants tended to dismember France, that all the Protestants were noblemen etc., etc. Hence the absurd conclusion that Paris and St. Bartholomew preserved the national unity, that Charles IX and the Guises performed the role of the Convention of 1793. This is a bizarre and eccentric paradox, displaying impartiality without sympathy, making a friend of our enemy, and utterly lacking in compassion for the slaughtered precursors of liberty. How odd it is to compare the assembly that defended France with the fanatical intrigue that delivered it up to a foreign power!

When the Protestants of the towns (the 25,000 in Toulouse, for example) fled desperately into the night with their children in their arms, when the tocsin rang out against them in the countryside, and the peasantry, armed by the priests, hunted them down in the woods, then, to be sure, scarcely any Protestants remained in the towns. To have done so would have necessitated a strong fortress. Those who would claim that the Protestants comprised an aristocracy belong themselves to the party of the murders. Moreover, in the 1562 rehearsal of St. Bartholomew, when the Parlement authorised the ringing of the Catholic tocsin, the names and professions of the unfortunates who perished reveal that they were workers. Rope-maker, bookseller, printer, pedlar, goldsmith, embroiderer—there is not a nobleman among them.

* * *

Armed with the weapons of criticism, I am now entering a forest of lies. I dare to proclaim with a genuine love of truth that I shall reestablish the true nature of the League, and I shall do so to the real advantage of that great Catholic party, which was so miserably deceived and became the plaything of its leaders. If I reveal my own blindness, I still protest my good faith.

A sound observer who was absent from Europe between the years 1780 and 1818 remarked: "This is no longer the same people. The France I knew in former times possessed a certain Savoyard character." I would add an Irish, and a Polish character, too. These old Catholic races may help us to guess the instinctive character of our ancestors—charming, brilliant, but lacking in gravity and capacity for reflexion.

Although the nation tended towards frivolity, it was none the less settled in its ways. Every endeavour towards improvement seemed to lack coherence and seriousness of purpose. It clung tenaciously to its way of life with a careless disregard for order and formality. The austere aspect of the Protestant party harmed it more than did anything else. Those stiff collars and starched ruffs (an economical means to cleanliness) were generally regarded as aristocratic pretentiousness. A petty clerk or bookseller who dressed himself thus incurred resentment. An *abbé* from those clerical institutions which were laws unto themselves would not have had to walk in sandals or proclaim his unwashed state to secure the adoration of the crowds. There was no personal pride in such men: all that the "good monk" had to say would be willingly heard.

We have seen the popularity of the worst of the hooded brethren in the streets of Paris. This democracy received an additional piece of Spanish filth when Toledo sent Loyola here, ostensibly to study. The crazed Italian mountebanks, such as that Panigarola whom the Pope sent on the eve of St. Bartholomew, also supposedly to study, were even more popular when they performed on public platforms. A certain extravagant mixture of cynical coarseness and pedantic affectation amused the people. The first of this kind was Auger, who deserted his profession as a juggler to become a scullion for the Jesuits, and was fished out from among the saucepans by Loyola, the fisher of men. Loyola coached him, made him into a pedant, and launched him on his new career. His successes were unbelievable: everything he said was believed. One of his sermons at Bordeaux delighted the church hierarchy, and persuaded them to conduct their own St. Bartholomew. Another sermon, at Issoire, converted 1500 men of Auvergne. Henry III, always seeking to please, said that he would have no other confessor, and gave him the laborious task of cleansing the royal conscience. He was the first of that royal dynasty of Jesuit confessors in the line of Cotton, Tellier and La Chaise.

The ability *to have believed whatever was said* was power itself. On the 24th August 1572 *it was believed* that Montmorency and a force of cavalry were coming to Paris to aid Coligny and to massacre the citizens. This was the clever lie that determined the issue on St. Bartholomew's day. On the 25th of August *the belief* that a thorn bush had flowered for a second time was taken to indicate the joy of Heaven and divine approval for the carnage of the preceding day. All the church bells of Paris pealed in unison to celebrate the miracle, and so signalled the resumption and extension of the massacre. At the end of 1575 *it was believed* that Montmorency-Damville was coming from the south with a great army to burn everything within twenty leagues of Paris, and that he demanded from the King a fearful punishment for the people of Paris. This ingenious fiction, which no historian has hitherto mentioned, explains the ease with which the terrified scum of Paris were persuaded to sign their adherence to the League. The most miraculous achievement was to make them believe that the League, whose existence they had seen and experienced for the past fifteen or twenty years, had actually first been inaugurated in that year, 1576.

Let us go back to the venerable origins of the League. At a very early stage the clergy had felt that our French monarchy, violent and capricious as it was, would not have the same terrible steadfastness of purpose evidenced by the Spanish crown. The priest-led rabble of March 5th 1559 had cried out, when the royal police obstructed its intentions: "We shall kill the King himself if we have to." These were effectively the first words of the League.

Like the monarchy, the Parlement vacillated between mildness and cruelty. A few of the magistrates were charitable men, as were the Séguiers and Harlays about the year 1558. The men of the gown tended to be unstable. In a massacre of St. Bartholomew an attorney who commanded the court's guards would not participate in the killing because he had "not yet worked himself up into a sufficient state of anger." The Catholic nobility was no more dependable. Vigor, the leader of the massacre, complained: "Our nobility does not want to strike down our enemies. . . . God will have this bastard nobility overwhelmed by the commonalty."

The clergy was far more confident of its ability to carry through its intentions. When in 1561 the King desired to have an inventory made of clerical wealth, his first words were assumed to imply the sale of church property, and the clergy, assembled in Notre-Dame, was moved to take its most decisive act. This first step was also the last, for it involved an appeal for civil and foreign war. On one hand it placed itself under the protection of the King of Spain: on the other it addressed itself to Guise. That sovereign captain of the party, of whom mention is made in the act of 1576, had appeared in the proceedings of fifteen years before. The first declaration of the League was made in May 1561.

The death of François de Guise seemed a hindrance, but nothing was really lost thereby, and everything was arranged at leisure. The role of the future captain, Henri de Guise, was prepared by concentrating within the Guise family a vast reserve of money, including the revenues of fifteen bishoprics, and, later of five provincial governorships. The first treasury of the League consisted of the means to nourish a great household and to buy bravos and German mercenaries. The League did not amount to much in the country, but it was very important within a large town. Paris was controlled in masterly fashion. The associations of artisans provided the League with a hold on the city. The light troops of the movement, the monks whose actions were somewhat unpredictable, were not enough to set the associations in motion. For this the regular work of the powerful Parisian diocese and its parish priests were needed. It is only necessary to contemplate the formidable edifice of Notre-Dame, and to know of its origins, to understand what was afoot. In the middle ages its foundations had been built on the ruins of the Albigenses, the Jews and the Templars, and its attitude to Protestantism in the sixteenth century was clear.

Gondi, the brother of that comte de Retz who was the principal counsellor of the Massacre of St. Bartholomew, was elevated to the Parisian episcopacy. A skilled group of the most vehement preachers was selected for the parish pulpits. From one generation to the next their violence mounted. The furious Vigor, the *curé* of Saint-Paul, was a veritable lamb in comparison with his disciples. Prévôt of Saint-Séverin trained the incomparable Boucher, *curé* of Saint-Benoît, in invective. The Gascon Guincestre, *curé* of Saint-Gervais, surpassed all these illustrious models, for, suiting his actions to his words, he roused the stupefied crowd by standing beside the altar and driving a dagger into the heart of a doll representing Henry III. On the right bank of the Seine the pulpits of Saint-Paul, Saint-Gervais, Saint-Leu and Saint-Germain-l'Auxcrois called down thunder and lightning. On the left bank roared the pulpits of Saint-Benoît, Saint-Séverin, Saint-Côme and Saint-André-des-Ares. Such were the organs of the League's propaganda.

These activities began twenty years earlier than the date assigned to them. They began well before St. Bartholomew, though doubtless with less coordination than was later achieved. The loosing of these little serpents long preceded the deaths of Henri de Guise and of Henry III, the martyr of Jacques Clément, when the whole nest of vipers suddenly burst into vituperation.

It is commonly supposed that the main purpose of this campaign was to satirise the King. This is broadly true. Poncet, the entertaining *curé* of Saint-Pierre-des-Arcis, and several others repeated buffooneries about him which greatly amused their audience. But it can be perceived that deeper and more political elements were cleverly intermingled with these tragi-comical ravings. The things that were vital to the League were repeated over and over again: that Saint Bartholomew was a revenge for Protestant excesses; that the Catholic League was also a reaction against, and an imitation of, Protestant leagues. So often was this said that more than one historian repeats it today. A well-cultivated lie, long repeated in chorus by half a million men, becomes a true fact.

The League was in no way an imitation. It had its own original and distinctive characteristics. The principal differences may readily be listed:

1. The Protestant unions were the defensive acts of a slaughtered minority which united its forces to prevent further slaughter. The League was an offensive association of a murderous majority which protested against the removal of the knife from its grasp.

2. One aspect that was quite peculiar to the League, and completely foreign to the Protestant associations which it is alleged to resemble, was the intimidation and persecution by denunciation of neutral and peacefully-inclined men. He who failed to join the League was regarded as an enemy; he who left it as a traitor, liable to punishment in person and in property.

3. The captain of the League was not simply a military leader, as were Condé and Coligny, who never assumed judicial power and allowed the ministers and the army to follow their own judicial procedures. This Catholic captain, in the terms

of the constitutive act of the League, was a kind of supreme judge who could proceed against those guilty of failing to join the League, and could punish those Leaguers who quarrelled among themselves.

4. The liberties of the provinces were to be restored to them by the League, in the forms in which they had existed at the time of Clovis. This was a direct appeal to local independence which the Protestants, who are so often accused of federation, never formulated. Their seclusion, and their demand for fortress towns to guarantee peace treaties, were purely defensive measures. They walled themselves in as much as they could, but this was only to survive. On the other hand, the restoration of local privileges, promised in the name of a vast Catholic majority, which no necessity or danger constrained to do so, meant but one thing: the destruction of national unity and a call to dissolution.

The Massacre of St. Bartholomew: Reason of State and Ideological Conflict

JEAN HÉRITIER

The literary historian, Jean Héritier, was born in 1892. He began his detailed studies of Renaissance France at the age of seventeen and in 1934 issued his study of Mary Queen of Scots and the murder of Darnley, which won the Prix Thérouanne of the French Academy. Following in the steps of Balzac, and relying on the specialized work of professional historians, he published his popular rehabilitation of Catherine de Medici in 1940. There were forty-four issues of this edition before the circumstances of the German occupation prevented further publication. Héritier's highly stylized biography has been criticized for the extent to which it depicts the Queen Mother as a conscious disciple of Machiavelli. It is also M. Héritier's intention to represent Catherine de Medici as a patriot, who, despite occasional mistakes, worked consistently and pragmatically to preserve French unity among the conflicting ideological forces of the period. M. Héritier is also the author of a biography of her contemporary, the Chancellor, Michel de L'Hospital.

THERE IS A LIMIT to a policy of compassion and to respect for the ideas and lives of individuals — the public good. Catherine de Medici had too good a head on her shoulders to forget it. To the end she would defend freedom of conscience — not in theory — for her intelligence was intensely pragmatical and by that fact political and highly disciplined to the changing complexities of the lives of nations — but in practice. As the Calvinists refused to enter into the bosom of the Church, to which almost the whole French nation remained faithful, it was politically wise to allow them to attend their sermons and to treat them in all other respects similarly to the remainder of the kingdom's subjects. But the right to hold prayer-meetings did not include the right to rebellion, since in the domain of conscience these heretical sub-

From Jean Héritier, *Catherine de Medici*, translated by Charlotte Haldane (New York, 1963), pp. 312–330. Reprinted by permission of Librairie Arthème Fayard and St. Martin's Press.

jects had been justly dealt with, the freedom that they had demanded having been granted, confirmed and guaranteed. As an insurgent Coligny was a criminal of State, and for reasons of State, on higher grounds, namely those of the public welfare.

Madame Catherine was too deeply imbued with the legal tradition not to realize how irregular it would be to have recourse a second time to the King's killer in order to strike down Coligny, without trial, after he had been amnestied, pardoned and reestablished in all his posts and honours. Charles IX was under the Admiral's influence and would never allow him to be re-arraigned. It was therefore necessary that Coligny should die at the hand of a murderer. The Queen Mother was not cruel, as she had proved time and time again. Historians may leave to her libellers the legend of an imaginary Medici who delighted in availing herself of poison. But if she was not cruel neither was Catherine tenderhearted. She could be hard, and could watch torturings as calmly as she was prepared to risk her own life in the trenches of Rouen and Le Havre. She had studied Machiavelli sufficiently closely to agree with him that cruelty could be ill or well used: "It can be said to be well employed (if one may call evil, good) when it is used on one occasion only, dictated by the necessity of retaining power, and on condition that one has no further recourse to it except in the interests of the nation."

In the present case there was no doubt where the interests of the nation lay. Coligny was ready to unleash a disastrous war. By temperament, character, predilection and necessity Madame Catherine was for compromise. But Coligny would not compromise; the completely free debates in the Council proved his use of intimidation. To endow the Governess of France with any form of modern liberalism is as contrary to historical fact as to psychological and ethical truth, but it is equally contrary to both to represent her as a second Agrippina. Her passion for power was as one with her love for the Crown of France. In his astonishing essay on Catherine de Medici, in which romanticism often goes hand in hand with an extraordinary intuition, leading in its essence to historical truth, Balzac put into this princess's mouth a phrase which expresses her completely: "You are all inclined to weep over a couple of hundred clodhoppers, sacrificed incidentally, those tears that you refuse to shed for the misfortunes of a whole generation, a century, or a world."

Reasons of State justified the death of the impenitent rebel, but it was not to be known that it was Catherine who struck the blow. Catherine cunningly gave thought to that revenge being everywhere demanded by the Guises for the assassination of François, ordered by Coligny. Let the Admiral be killed by the Lorraines and Protestant fury turn on them, whose ambition was no less a threat to the State than Coligny's fanaticism. The Guises against the Châtillons — what did it concern the Queen? The revenge of the Lorraines would surprise her at a moment when she herself was entirely taken up with the Béarnais wedding. Once again the royal wisdom would have been impotent, but this time only in appearance. In reality, with Coligny out of the way and the Guises massacred as a reprisal, the field would be clear for the King, freed from the dangerous leaders of both factions, to proceed with his task of pacification.

. . . Excellently organized as the plot had been, it failed utterly because Maurevert missed the Admiral. . . . The old fox, brave as usual, and completely in command of himself, was not for one moment in doubt as to the instigators of the attack, Catherine and the Guises, all the more so as the musket, abandoned by Maurevert, belonged to one of Monsieur's bodyguards. As soon as he received the news, Charles IX burst into a rage. The Queen Mother instantly summed up the extent and seriousness of the consequences of this abortive attack. The Admiral would demand and obtain from Charles IX without any difficulty an inquiry and a trial which would reveal the truth. Catherine knew her son too well not to be sure that whilst he would not dare to touch her in one of his usual rages, he would kill his brother, the Duc d'Anjou, with his own hand. As for herself, the Admiral would be sufficiently persuasive to obtain her exile. If Coligny were dead no one in the world would have been capable of turning Charles IX against his mother, and she, playing on his hatred of Henri de Guise, could easily have directed his anger towards him. But living, Coligny would turn it on Catherine and Anjou. How to divert that fury from themselves? This was the question that the Queen Mother now asked herself in the greatest anguish. For the first time in her life she panicked.

. . . Later on there was a romanticized version of all this [the background of the massacre] based on the *Stratageme* of Capilupi, gaps in the correspondence of the Nuncio, Salviati, and the views of Çuniga, Petrucci, Cavriana, and Cavalli; a collection of all the different opinions contained in contemporary memoirs. Some of them spoke of premeditation on the part of the Queen Mother, and even — which is absurd — attributed a monstrous kind of Machiavellism to Charles IX, quite contrary to his impulsive character and attacks of rage. Others claimed that there was a Protestant plot. But we should not, after all, forget that the documents only reveal fragments of the truth. Even the most considered of them only report a small part of what was said and done and they reflect the ideas, feelings and wishes of their authors. In reading the thousands of pages written around the attack on Coligny and Marguerite's wedding, which became known as the Ruddy Wedding, one would become giddy did one not remember the essential point — Catherine was Queen; she was also a woman and a mother.

As Queen she had proved her devotion to France, her understanding of the permanent interests of the State, her constant determination to sacrifice everything to the public welfare. As a woman she had a passion for power, as others have for love; she was filled entirely with what the Venetians so happily call *l'affetto di signoreggiare.* As a mother she saw that her son Charles had shaken off her tutelage, and that her son Anjou, her favourite, an accomplice in the attack that had failed, stood in danger of death owing to his elder brother's hatred. Her nerves had given way and she was distraught. But we know that in Catherine de Medici the instinct of self-preservation quickly overcame her fears. This instinct of self-preservation now showed her what line to take; she must re-assert her authority over the King and there was only one means of doing so, by terror, in order to forestall the inevitable terrorism of the Admiral's avengers and the counter-terrorism of the Guisards. Knowing that the Huguenots were determined on revenge, Paris was about to rise, for the agents of the Guises were busily spreading their propaganda. What decision should she take? In her gardens of the Tuileries the Queen consulted her Italians — Nevers, Gondi, Birague, on whose personal devotion she could completely rely, and Tavannes, who seemed strong enough to rally the Parisians round the throne. But as the day advanced her danger grew and Catherine was still seeking a solution. She really was like a trapped fox now and in these circumstances Machiavelli could provide her neither with guidance nor help.

But suddenly circumstances brought the Queen Mother this help, which had seemed so completely beyond reach that on that Saturday evening of August 23rd at her supper-table a gentleman from Gascony, Pardaillan, dared to shout in her face that if the King did not do so the Huguenots would furnish their own justice. Two Calvinist noblemen, Bouchavannes, who had always remained loyal to her, and Gramont, during the course of the day, came to tell her that at the Admiral's lodgings there had been a meeting resulting in the decision to attempt a *coup de force,* that the Queen and her children were to be killed, and even the King of Navarre as well, because he was suspected of only being a lukewarm adherent of the Religion. Bouchavannes' and Gramont's accusation is a fact, confirmed by all the despatches of the ambassadors. But was this accusation based on firm grounds or was it the work of *agents-provocateurs?* Did Catherine genuinely believe in the existence of this plot? Or did she use it as an excuse? God alone knows.

Thanks to the revelations of Bouchavannes and Gramont, whether they were true or false, Catherine now had a means of influencing Charles IX in order to obtain an order from him without which nothing could be done — the order to massacre the leaders of a new Amboise conspiracy before they would have time to act. This time they were too strong to be put down. It was a question of timing — the Huguenots must at all costs be forestalled. . . . As the threatened Calvinist Vespers remain merely hypothetical this cannot be confirmed historically. But we do know that the inquiry had been opened, that Coligny was the King's master and that, in consequence, had she not struck first, Catherine would have been lost and France given over to civil war by the revolt of the Catholics against the King, who was allied to the Protestants. Catherine staged a killing in order not to be killed herself. Apart from this, which is certain, everything else is mere supposition and history cannot concern itself with suppositions but can only take events into account, which is the only way to try to understand what happened. The cause of Saint Bartholomew was fortuitous — Maurevert's clumsiness. On that point the opinions of the diplomats are unanimous and Çuniga [the Spanish ambassador] summed it up: "As the musket-shot was badly aimed and as the Admiral knew whence it came, they determined to do what they did."

This was the true cause of the Matins of Paris. The commentaries that can be quoted on them stem from moralizing and apologetics, but not from history. Saint Bartholomew, like Wassy, like the two Michelades, was an unpremeditated massacre. We do not say a spontaneous massacre — spontaneity does not occur in history any more than in biology. Catherine de Medici decided on Saint Bartholomew because she could not do otherwise. She considered herself to be acting on grounds of legitimate defence. According to the spirit and customs of the period her right to put the Admiral to death is beyond discussion. It also included the right to kill the Admiral's avengers, since they were the accomplices of a State criminal. Catherine de Medici decided on the massacre of his accomplices because she had failed to murder their leader. In one case as in the other it was an execution of rebels, but an execution that required the King's authority. It was exclusively aimed at the great noblemen — Coligny, La Rochefoucauld, Téligny, Caumont La Force, Montgomery, and a few others. With Paris under arms such a surprise attack, by depriving the Huguenots of their chiefs, would render them impotent. But in this, Catherine's reasoning was at fault, and did not show her usual clarity of mind. Bloodshed provokes bloodshed and all preventative terrorism is a worse remedy than the evil it is designed to cure. Terrorism is only efficacious as a means of repression. Given the state of overexcitement of the Parisian masses, the massacre of the leaders would inevitably lead to general carnage. . . .

Catherine de Medici and her Italians did not know Paris very well, with its impulsiveness and feverishness. Tavannes was a military man who knew nothing about the bourgeois militia and the populace of a capital. Charles IX, sombre and rigid in his weakling's pride, wanting to prove to his mother and brother that he was not afraid of the Huguenots, was in command under Catherine's directions. He did not concern himself with the consequences; he was the master and he would show them that he was. At three o'clock in the morning the bell of the Palace of Justice would give the signal for the executions. Everything had been foreseen for the maintenance of order — the closing of the gates, with the Huguenots' troops encamped in the suburbs; the bourgeois militia was to occupy the squares, crossroads and quays; the artillery was stationed on the Place de Grève. . . . Everything had been foreseen except one thing—Claude Marcel was not going to use his thugs to reinforce the bourgeois militia of Le Charron, but to exterminate all the Protestants of Paris. Claude Marcel was the Guise's man, a fanatical Catholic, and at the same time enjoyed the Queen Mother's confidence. As others were to kill the great noblemen he would take it on himself to kill the rest of the heretics. He was not concerned with Machiavellism. He was a goldsmith who had become a municipal magistrate but there was nothing of the Benvenuto Cellini about him and he did not go into Florentine subtleties. He ordered his men to make certain that not one blasphemer be spared. *Le Roi le veut.* Those were the King's orders.

Thus were extra-legal executions to be transformed into the Matins of Paris.

. . . Saint Bartholomew thus took its place in the long series of atrocities, both Catholic and Protestant, that for twelve years had devastated the realm, and in magnitude surpassed them all. Those Matins of Paris were the proof of the failure of the Queen Mother's policy. She had no doubts whatever of her right to condemn Coligny and the other leading rebel noblemen to death. But events proved that she had deluded herself when she had endeavoured to prevent a possible Huguenot retaliation for the abortive attack on the Admiral. There are times when it is preferable to endure an attack instead of launching one.

On August 24, 1572, Paris proved to Catherine that she had made a mistake. What she had always tried to avoid, what Spain and the Holy See had in vain urged her to do, to exterminate the Huguenots, had now been done by her own fault. And as the result of that extermination she had become the prisoner of the Catholic party, of Philip II and the Pope. The anti-Protestant organizations in Paris had drawn up lists of heretics and these provided the grounds for a methodical massacre such as occurs in all revolutionary riots — an appalling law of history and one in which there is, alas, no exception, to whatever ideological or mystical creeds the rival camps may belong. There is no such thing as spontaneous terrorism or anarchy. With the aid of carefully drawn-up lists of suspects such matters are always prepared in advance by agitators. In fact Catherine de Medici had handed Paris over to Catholic democracy. The Matins of Paris were the distant forerunner of the League.

. . . Whatever may be the case with regard to the number of dead, it was a fact that Royalty was once again reduced to impotence. Impotent wisdom was succeeded by mad impotence; the situation was infinitely more serious, for the sovereign had destroyed his own powers of arbitration.

Catherine, Gallican and anti-Spanish, was faced with the ruin and wreckage of her policy of public welfare. The Emperor and Elizabeth of England, on whom she had based such splendid hopes of an alliance, were against her. Switzerland, the Northern monarchies, Poland, Turkey, understood at once that the King of France had lost control of his subjects and no longer counted. All the diplomatic despatches, those sent by the French Government after the Matins of Paris, in which the contradictions and lies are obvious, as well as those it received, in which the diplomatic style in usage barely concealed their underlying contempt, expose the confusion of the Queen Mother and her legislators. Just as, in spite of her repeated orders, she had been unable to stop the massacre, so now she was unable to delude anyone. The Huguenots threw over the fiction in which they had sincerely believed, of the rebellion being linked with loyalty to the King. The correspondence, letters and libels on the Protestant side no longer distinguished between the King and the enemies of the Religion. As Hauser said very well, Saint Bartholomew

> had given an impetus to all the democratic possibilities inherent in Calvinism in spite of

itself and against Calvin's will. What John Knox did in Scotland, what the Netherlands ministers were doing under William the Silent, was happening in France and in French circles in Geneva. . . . And, a natural reversal of values, at the moment when Protestant polemics became republican (or at any rate *patriotic* according to the meaning of this word in the Low Countries) Catholic polemics withdrew from opposing and began to confuse the rights of the Prince and the right of God. That is how France, the scene of the most tragic episodes in the religious war, became the centre of European political ideology and of irreconcilable conflicts.

The battle on which Catherine had insisted had ended in disaster. Indomitable fighter that she was, she first of all covered her retreat. She had gambled and lost; now she paid up, without arguing. She went over to the victors. Machiavellism had failed her because she was a woman and a mother before she was a politician. Faced with the domestic tragedy of her sons' mutual hatred and the submission of the elder to Coligny, the Queen had given way to the woman. Yet Machiavellism was an instrument that should not be discarded. Since violence adopted for reasons of State had only made the situation worse, it was better to resort to perfidy. Catherine pulled herself together with her usual will-power. She would lie to everyone and she would not be believed — that she knew. Nevertheless, behind this smoke-screen of lies that she would spread over the battlefield on which she had been beaten, the Florentine Queen would be able to retreat in order to prepare her rehabilitation.

Her genius for dissimulation and deceit was now to be given full rein. From a moral point of view it was a sorry spectacle, but for the historian and politician one more fascinating than ever. "Princes who adapt their behaviour to a given situation," said Machiavelli,

> are seldom unlucky and Fortune only changes for those who do not know how to conform to their times. . . . Also, circumstances determine whether or not a prince had behaved well or badly on such an occasion. There are times when extreme caution is necessary, others when the prince must be prepared to take a chance, but nothing is more difficult than to change one's conduct or character at the right moment, either because we are unable to give up our habits and inclinations or else because we cannot decide to give up a course that has always served us well.

The moment had come to give up the course of the policy of compassion and to howl with those wolves whom one had made the mistake of unleashing. After the shock of the Matins of Paris, the Huguenots were for a time routed, of no account, lacking cadres and reduced to sterile fury and threats. And for the time being also the Catholics, now Guisards, Spaniards and Papists, could not be brought back to obedience. Madame Catherine would follow the same line; she too would also become a fine and thorough exterminator of heretics. . . .

The Catholic League: Popular Revolution and Fanaticism

JEAN-BAPTISTE-HONORÉ CAPEFIGUE

Jean-Baptiste-Honoré Capefigue (1802–1872) was one of the most prolific and widely-read of French historians writing in the second and third quarters of the nineteenth century. A qualified archivist-paleographer, Capefigue pursued the profession of journalism. His historical and biographical works on sixteenth-century France won him a laureate from the *Académie des inscriptions et belles-lettres* of the Institute. The present extract is taken from his eight-volume history of the period of the Wars of Religion. In his description of the League, Capefigue compares the ferment of popular passions with earlier periods of anarchy and also with the French Revolution.

IN THE HIERARCHIC ORDER of authority the municipal council of Paris, the city council comprising the mayor [*prévôt*] and the aldermen, controlled public administration, commanded the bourgeois militia, regulated the markets and assembled the masters of the guilds. All instructions for law enforcement and good order came from the municipal government. The people might carefully have chosen magistrates who were devout Catholics and members of the Holy League, and, indeed, the council of 1588 was composed of bourgeois sound in faith and prominent in city affairs. And yet the council contained conservative men of property who were unwilling to vary a fixed administrative system.

Beside the government of the commune another government was formed — by nature more dynamic and forceful. Paris was divided into sixteen quarters, and at the head of each was an elected representative [*quartenier*] of the people. He tended to be a tradesman and a member of the bourgeois militia, often holding the rank of colonel. These sixteen *quarteniers* formed a special council, independent of the Hôtel de Ville in the place de Grève, and dominating its resolutions through the knowledge that behind them lay the power of the people in arms. Its meetings served as a forum for orators of extreme views. The most powerful among them was the eloquent Senault, a simple Parisian advocate. He became a kind of Roman tribune when he discussed some measure at the council with which he did not agree. If he observed that it received general approbation and was about to be decided, he would announce in a loud voice:

"Gentlemen I shall not allow it: I oppose it on behalf of forty thousand men." At which all present would bow their heads like so many puppets, and would not utter another word [L'Estoile].

Among demagogues whose talents and influence were not so great were the commissary Louchart, and Esmonnot, an attorney at the Parlement. Both enjoyed the capricious favour of the markets. The man of action among them was Jean Leclerc, another attorney at the court of the Parlement, who after his election as captain of his quarter, had become an expert with the arquebus and the dagger. Leclerc was en-

From J.-B.-H. Capefigue, *Histoire de la Réforme, de la Ligue et du règne de Henri IV* (Paris, 1834), vol. V, pp. 196–200, vol. VI, pp. 407–410, vol. VIII, pp. 410–413. [Editor's translation.]

trusted with all the commune's plans involving violence. At the head of the bourgeois guard he governed the Bastille in Saint-Antoine, organised the night watch and arrested luke-warm Catholics or traitors. Leclerc was better known in the Paris markets than the King of France himself.

The difference between these two councils was that the Hôtel de Ville represented the Catholic bourgeois element in the League, favouring order and a systematic administration, while the council of the Sixteen represented the artisans and their associations, an element encouraging anarchy at every street corner.

Such were the purely municipal authorities. In a more general sense the Parlement, with its political sessions, its presidencies and its sympathy for the monarchical tradition, must also be considered. Since popular opinion believed in the ancient origin of its authority, and since this authority extended beyond the walls of Paris, the Parlement was obliged to play an active role. In its existing state the Parlement could not be relied on to support the League, for it contained too much support for the crown. It was known that some of the presidents and judges had been in touch with Henry III, the deposed tyrant, and might betray the city and the Holy League itself. A violent reform was needed, and the people of Paris were later to attempt it. The other sovereign courts were less important and the League was less concerned to take control of them. In other respects these courts were loyal enough to the League.

The Sorbonne composed the principal ecclesiastical authority. The Sorbonne could be relied upon. It supported the principles of Catholic government, just as the Parlement supported the traditions of judicial and administrative procedures. The Parisian *curés* also played a significant role. In every church and parish there were preachers in close touch with the Sorbonne and ready to use their pulpits to proclaim its views to the people. The Sorbonne was in complete understanding with the council of the Sixteen. It contained the same opinions and the same enthusiasm for the League.

The nature of all these authorities was essentially municipal. Their power was confined to the city. The other towns had a certain respect for Paris, but they did not recognise its council as anything more than a single member of a general confederation. A need existed for a higher authority in the form of a provisional government with power over the League as a whole. The council of the Catholic Union, which had previously been a somewhat mysterious and occasional authority, then publicly proclaimed its permanent powers. It took control of the supreme direction of the movement and loudly demanded the deposition of Henri de Valois. Denunciation of tyranny, public prayers and the formulae of the Parlement no longer met the situation. The people demanded the deposition of Henry III. Thus the Holy League created a kind of interim political administration, while awaiting some settled measure which would follow the formal deposition of the King.

* * *

The municipal and Catholic government of Paris lasted for five years [1588–1593] and its history was full of life and emotion. The way was paved for the restoration of Henry IV when this phase in the vast popular drama of the markets and the associations of the artisans had ended. It might be said that the popular movement itself brought about the restoration. Such a movement has served its purpose when popular opinion believes it to have done so, and enlightened opinion desires its conclusion. At the end of 1593, after the conversion of the King of Navarre, the League no longer had any serious purpose in the eyes of the bourgeois, and inevitably it slipped into a decline which led to its ultimate ruin. The entry of Henry IV to Paris was an inevitable fact. The issue was no longer that of Catholicism, but rather that of Spain. The entire vast religious movement that resisted the triumph of the Béarnais had been transformed into an intrigue, and the intrigue collapsed in face of the general interest of society.

A close examination of the different phases of the popular revolution whose details I have just retraced, reveals various differences in emphasis that divide it into phases. After the barricades all classes of the population participated in the movement. The expulsion of the King from Paris and the organisation of a broad municipal movement were welcomed with great enthusiasm. The entire bourgeoisie shared the opinions of the lower classes of the markets. The Hôtel de Ville acted, arming the citizens and defending the ramparts. The popular representatives of the quarters called out the people, who brought forth their arquebuses and long culverins in the service of their faith and their city.

In the second period, the bourgeoisie grew tired. Their momentary energy was dissipated as selfish interests made themselves felt. The bourgeois had created a riot: they had not desired a revolution. The men of the Parlement, at first associated with the popular movement, placed themselves at the head of this mixed body of opinion. At this point the overtures of the third party for peace were begun, and the Catholics regarded them as treason. There followed the forceful and bloody measures of the Sixteen, which were an expression of the fervour and devotion of the multitude. This was the democratic period of the League. The people were master of all authority, and exercised it with violence. Thenceforth there were instances of energetic resistance, and the war became one of courage and fanaticism.

The Duke of Mayenne, who had placed himself at the head of the faction of the bourgeoisie and the Parlement, came to the aid of the middle class. With the help of his gentlemen-at-arms he made ready a kind of counter-revolution which supported the moderate spirits and the merchant class against the ardour of the people. Several of the Sixteen were handed over to the executioner. The municipal council chose new leaders and accepted the influence of moderate ideas. The League still existed. The towns remained united by powerful bonds. But the people were no longer in control. It accepted the authority of others and no longer acted as the directing force.

* * *

There were similarities between this period and other epochs, especially in the twelfth and thirteenth centuries. But in this period a more strongly municipal trend was evident, a movement directed more energetically in the interests of the middle and lower classes. The associations of artisans dominated the League, and formed that alliance which always results from the association of the clergy with the lower classes in Catholic countries — an alliance between the material force of labour and the persuasive influence of the holy gospel. The League had the effect of imprinting a stronger spirit of liberty upon the commune, and of awaking within it that ferment of popular independence which we have seen breaking forth in Paris in the barricades of 1588, in the organisation of the Sixteen, and in the sovereign alliance of cities with cities.

While it was based upon the moral ideals of Catholicism, the League had also to adopt secular doctrines based on the various powers it contained. Submission to princes was in all respects subordinate to submission to the Church. An excommunicated king could not legally govern his subjects. Thence arose the doctrines of regicide and the unbridled demagogy of Leaguer pamphlets. Government no longer assumed the form of monarchy. It mattered little whether the League turned itself into a monarchy or a republic. Its principle was that of Catholicism, and, provided that this was respected, the form of government was merely an accessory issue on which the Church did not trouble itself. This explains the anarchic doctrines preached from the pulpits of the League. Paris could be governed by a king or by the Sixteen, but this was not the vital question. There was no other public law save the supremacy of the Pope, the ancient basis of society.

In this connexion I believe that the League fostered the growth of municipal independence. If it had succeeded in creating its own king it would have imposed popular limitations upon him, and the union of the multitude with the Church would have constituted a religious democracy that would have prevented the deviations of absolute power. All these street disorders, this shattering of monarchical unity, these associations with foreign powers in which peoples negotiated with kings and kings negotiated with peoples, weakened faith in the institution of monarchy. When the King of Spain wrote to the municipalities or to the councils of the cities of Paris, Lyon, or Marseille, he was negotiating with veritable republics. The towns managed to preserve the memory of these transactions, when citizens had dealt with kings on a basis of equality. A tribunate was created in the pulpit, and highly theocratic doctrines thundered forth from it against the preeminence of the crown. Was there any real difference between the regicidal jeers of the Leaguer pamphlets that animated popular passions and the most fiery journals of another period, when equal sport was made with the heads of kings? Religious fanaticism found praise for the dagger that reached the heart of Henry III, just as political fanaticism later had its hymns to those who caused princes to mount the scaffold.

Finally, in all this confusion an advance took place in the development of ideas. Liberty assumed unbridled, indeed highly destructive, forms, but it remained a fine and powerful means of intellectual progress. The struggle between two faiths sharpened the edge of controversy and provided new scope for the exercise of the higher powers of the human mind. Clearer views of the relations between crown and subject emerged, and there was close examination of the rights of each, including the limitations of power and the rules that the sovereign authority should impose upon itself. Everything came under discussion, and principles were enunciated with greater precision when they were all subjected to the light of reason. Nothing is new in the history of the human spirit. All events resemble each other because man is their originator, and, though mankind may modify itself, it does not change. It would be interesting to compare the natures of the two periods presented to us. One was produced by the energy of the religious principle; the other by the effervescence and the power of liberty. The causes alone were different. Both displayed equally strange peculiarities and exerted an equally powerful effect upon the future.

The Catholic League: Popular Insurrection as the Instrument of Aristocracy and Clergy

PAUL ROBIQUET

Paul Robiquet (1848–1928) held a doctorate in law as well as in letters. He was a prominent lawyer during the Third Republic, who devoted much of his time to the municipal history of Paris. In his history of Paris during the League, his conservative inclinations persuaded him to oppose the belief that the popular insurrections of the time were anticipations of democracy. In the following extract he argues that the forces of popular revolution were adroitly managed by the ultra-Catholic nobility and clergy.

LATE IN 1584 Charles Hotmann, known as La Rocheblond, had collaborated with Prévost (curé of Saint-Séverin), Boucher (curé of Saint-Benoît) and Mathieu de Lannoy (canon of Soissons) to establish the bases of the League's organisation. By 1588 the revolutionary cadres had been greatly strengthened in size and efficiency. It has already been noted that the first four conspirators had made many recruits, among whom mention has been made of the advocate Louis d'Orléans, Jean Pelletier, curé of Saint-Jacques, the merchant Compans, Jean Guincestre, a bachelor of theology, Bussy le Clerc, an attorney at the Parlement, the commissary Louchart, the notary la Morlière, the attorney Crucé and many other fanatics. The higher direction of the party had been entrusted to a council of nine or ten persons, both clerical and lay; but effective authority belonged to the Council of Six, which was actually a controlling committee, since the Six managed all the others. The Six were charged with responsibilities in the sixteen districts of the city. Crucé had to take particular responsibility for the districts near the university; Pelletier for Saint-Marcel and Saint-Germain; Compans was in charge of the Ile de la Cité; La Chapelle, Louchart and Bussy supervised the remaining districts. La Rocheblond was the other member of the committee of the Six. Sometimes they met in Boucher's room in the Sorbonne, or at the collège de Forteret, where Boucher later took lodgings and which was called "the cradle of the League." Sometimes they met at the house of La Rocheblond or at La Chapelle's. The first Leaguer conspirators had taken elaborate measures to observe secrecy, and, while they had actively spread propaganda against the King, they had revealed the mysteries of their organisation only to a very restricted number of reliable persons, "in such a way that at the beginning there were only five persons with the sieur de la Rocheblond who operated throughout the whole city to institute and establish the League" (*Dialogue du Maheustre et du Manant*).

If this was the composition of the General Staff of the League, something should be said of the particular classes of the Parisian population that provided its troops. In the first place the League could count upon the immense army of monks of various orders, whose abbeys seemed more like citadels for the insurrection, and whose dec-

From Paul Robiquet, *Paris et la Ligue sous le règne de Henri III* (Paris, 1886), pp. 299–304, 355–358, 577–581. [Editor's translation.]

lamations in the churches or even in the streets showed that in them the Guises possessed thousands of fanatical agents uninfluenced by material interests. Spanish gold proved a valuable aid to this clerical propaganda and aroused mercenary support among the lowest classes and the rabble who thronged the wharves along the Seine. With a virtual unanimity, inspired directly by Henry III's exactions from the Church and by hostility to any heretical prince, the clergy could design no better means to deprive Henry of Navarre of his hereditary rights to the crown than to suppress and overthrow the last Valois. The nobility itself was divided, but the gentlemen who followed the fortunes of the Guises daily became more numerous, for the exclusive favour that the King accorded his *mignons* deprived them of employment for their swords. Among the royal favourites several, such as Villequier and Villeroy imitated Catherine de Medici's double-faced political game, and negotiated with the leaders of the League. On the other hand, the Guises could count upon the constant zeal of their own officers, whom they paid well and never abandoned. There were similar divisions in the bourgeois class and the magistrature. It is true that the Parlement had little sympathy for the clergy. It had shown its temper by protesting against the bull of Sixtus V and the claim of the Pope to subordinate all crowns to the spiritual power. But the humiliations inflicted on them by Henry III, and the threats to their property and rank, had caused many of these members of the sovereign courts, who ought to have been the staunchest defenders of the monarchy, to defect to the opposition. Yet it was within this group of the men of the gown and the rich bourgeois that the Valois and later Henry of Navarre, still kept their most valuable partisans — even though their cooperation was paralyzed by a complete lack of direction. Finally, the defects of the royal administration, the incessant levying of taxes and the confiscation of the public bonds had provoked a lively resentment against the crown among poverty-stricken small rentiers and petty businessmen. The prestige of the Guises, together with the prejudices or beliefs of many sincere men, further swelled the number of unconscious accomplices of the League. Hence was derived its great strength in Paris — and its activities were extended to all parts of the country.

Emissaries, who were well provided with money and furnished with precise instructions, maintained liaison between the two councils of the League in Paris and the Catholic provincial centres. When an envoy from a town or province arrived in the capital, he always knew on what door to knock:

> for there were certain Catholics designated to receive the said agents according to the provinces whence they came — some for Picardy, others for Normandy, Burgundy, Orléans, Lyon and other towns and provinces. For there was much traffic with all these regions, and their agents returned well-informed and with copious written instructions and promises of mutual aid in the maintenance of the true religion against the heretics and those who abetted them (*Dialogue du Maheustre et du Manant*).

Thus at the time of his rupture with Henry III the duc de Guise controlled a powerful organisation which had already successfully defied the court in the seditions following the denunciation of the King in the pulpit of Saint-Séverin on 2nd September 1587. It was Guise himself who devised the plan of grouping the sixteen quarters of Paris into five general areas, so as to prevent the division of his forces and the sharing of confidential information among too many Leaguers. Moreover, since the Duke was not entirely certain of the support of the officers of the municipal militia, he introduced into its companies a certain number of gentlemen devoted to his interests. These included Urbain de Laval-de-Bois-Dauphin, Charles de Cossé, comte de Brissac, de Mayneville, de Gomeron, de Richebourg, Guedon d'Esclavolles de Chamois, and Antoine de Saint-Paul. Five hundred cavaliers, for whose command the duc d'Aumale was designated, were quartered in outlying districts near Paris, such as Aubervilliers, La Villette, Saint-Ouen and Saint-Denis. By the order of the duc de Guise a secret review of the forces of the League was arranged. The roll call provided a total of either 30,000 men (according to the report of the royalist spy, Nicolas Poulain) or 20,000 (according to the historian de Thou). This army of fanatics increased every day with the enrolment of the monks and all the adventurers in the Guises' clientèle. These irregulars were impelled to converge upon the capital by the promise of some impending enterprise. They comprised, according to the *Mémoires de la Ligue,* men "of every rank, with their arms and equipment, who entered this great city by divers ways and disappeared into it as in a vast sea, without being directly noticed or recognised in any way except by their own people." Thus all was prepared for the rising, and the first spark would fire the train.

* * *

[After the rising in the May 1588 "barricades" in Paris] Guise was master of the capital, but to what use would he turn his victory? Henry III had been chased out of Paris and humiliated by the League, but how could he make good his defeat? The Parisian municipality was disorganised: the city councillors Le Comte and Lugoly, who had played an active part on behalf of the regular municipal authority in opposing the insurrectional organisation of the League, were obliged to take refuge in flight because of their loyalty to the royal cause. The other two councillors, Bonnard and Saiinct-Yon, had maintained a most equivocal attitude during the rising and had become sympathetic to the League immediately it had secured the victory. Since they were regarded with suspicion by the clerical faction they found it necessary "to attest before heaven and earth that they were innocent of whatever they were charged with; that their colleagues had betrayed them and had consulted together in their absence without summoning them to be present." The mayor [*prévôt des marchands*] Hector de Pereuse, who had bravely stayed in Paris after the King's flight, was speedily arrested.

In this way the expulsion of the monarchy from the capital left the field open to a triumphant popular uprising. In 1588 the enemy of the crown was not just a single man, some Etienne Marcel, who had momentarily succeeded in stirring up the ignorant and fickle masses: it was the powerful association of a faction of the high nobility with almost all the clergy and with the most active section of the bourgeoisie. It consisted of a skilfuly contrived organisation, long since perfected and matured and set on foot by a group of clever and energetic conspirators. It was powerfully supported — one might even say dominated — by the complicity of the imperious Philip II. The revolution of May 1588 made a clean sweep not only of the royal government but also of the traditional municipal authority. It had no intention of giving to the mayoralty an extension of power that would make it virtually sovereign or completely autonomous. In 1358 the victor in the struggle with the central power had been the *prévôt des marchands,* Etienne Marcel, and after a fashion the revolution had assumed an almost exclusively municipal character. In 1588 the *prévôt des marchands* was included among the vanquished, and, if the core of the old institutions were not altered in appearances, the actual and complete municipal power passed to the councils of the League. Of course, it may be said that the duc de Guise and the Sixteen had written into their revolutionary programme "the reestablishment of the ancient freedom of municipal elections," but this was an illusion. Basically the League replaced a regular electoral system with tumultuous popular elections. There could be no greater freedom of choice than in the past, because choice was dictated by the leaders of a faction instead of by the King. In the last analysis the true aim, as, indeed, the true consequences, of the barricades was to hand over the government to the clergy and its followers. In modern terms it might be called the triumph of clericalism. History can leave no doubt as to the audacious intent of all those preachers who led the four hundred monks and eight hundred students whose role in the day of the barricades we have already described. On behalf of the people, as well as on behalf of the Pope, they invoked the right to depose the King. It was the duc de Guise who put this doctrine in their mouths. And yet it was Guise who held back at the last moment and allowed the escape of "the prey he held in his toils." Etienne Marcel had spared the dauphin Charles and had died for it: Henri de Guise spared King Henry III and he was to die for it also. A king who allows himself to be openly insulted by a subject has slight chance of retaining his crown; a subject "who draws his sword against his prince ought at once to throw away the scabbard." This was the observation of the Duke of Parma when he heard of the outcome of the barricades. For his part, the Pope blamed both Henri de Guise for having placed himself, after his arrival in the capital, in the power of a king he had so cruelly outraged, and Henry III for allowing the Duke to escape. "What a faint-hearted prince! What an unfortunate prince!" exclaimed Sixtus V, "for having lost the chance of ridding himself of a man who seemed born to destroy him." The duc de Guise, on his side, had first committed the enormous imprudence of proceeding almost alone to the Louvre, and had then committed a second, yet graver, imprudence when he allowed the defeated monarch to leave the capital. Half a rebellion makes nonsense, and "in truth, he who has once desired to drink the wine of the gods should never again acknowledge himself to be a man . . . for one must be Caesar or nothing" [L'Estoile].

* * *

At the news of the assassination of Henry III, Paris became delirious with joy. The city assumed a mourning habit of green, the livery of fools, as the diarist L'Estoile called it, and echoed the words of the duchesse de Guise and the duchesse de Montpensier: "The tyrant is dead. The race of Valois has been extinguished." Who was to fill the vacuum? Mayenne, Philip II, the Duke of Savoy, the Cardinal de Bourbon? No one knew. Basically the capital hated only one person, the heretical King of Navarre. And when the situation had been defined, when Mayenne, seeing the difficulty of crowning himself, had the old Cardinal de Bourbon proclaimed as Charles X, and had bestowed upon himself the title of Lieutenant-General of the state and crown of France, the city of Paris wrote to the Pope on 7th August, revealing within the space of a few lines its entire policy:

> This city, once so rich in all kinds of wealth, has reduced itself to poverty and to its present deplorable state through bearing alone the full burden of this just and necessary conflict. Nevertheless, it remains resolved to suffer fire and famine rather than yield to the rule of a heretic.

Paris subordinated everything to the religious issue. The League identified the cause of the Catholic religion with that of the state. It had had Henry III killed, not because he had dissipated the resources of the state and overtaxed his capital, not even because he had been regarded as a bad ruler, but solely "because he had ignored the threat of the divine vengeance of St. Peter." There could not have been a clearer declaration that Paris recognised the temporal supremacy of the Roman Pontiff. . . . It is understandable that certain historians, notably Capefigue, have described the League as "a municipal republic entirely devoted to Catholicism." But it might be added that this alleged government through municipalities was singularly oligarchic in its high command, for the authority of the princes of Lorraine overwhelmed the Hôtel de Ville in Paris. Basically, Mayenne was very much opposed to the tumultuous assertions of the popular masses, and he did not personally produce in them the extraordinary effects that his brother, the great Henri de Guise, had evoked. But, on the other hand, he endured, when he had to, the irresistible influence of religious passions and he also accepted the influence of Spain, which introduced the sombre spirit of the Inquisition into the counsels of the League.

The intervention of the Paris municipality in the dramatic sequence of events we have described should be reduced to its proper place. The Hôtel de Ville served as the instrument of the Guises to bring about the revolt of Paris against the King in the barricades of May 12th 1588, and, later, it was used to organise the civil war and to avenge the royal assassination of the Guises at Blois. Yet, basically, it played only a subordinate role. It is just as wrong to compare, as Capefique did, the revolution of 1588 with that of 1789 as it is to compare it with the great democratic and municipal movement of 1358. La Chapelle-Marteau, the leader of the League municipality, possessed neither the personality nor the high aspirations of Etienne Marcel. Like the other Parisian deputies at the Estates General at Blois he was merely the humble and ineffective agent of the duc de Guise. The whole organization of the movement was based on the alliance of the monastic orders, who were inspired by Rome and Spain, with the aristocratic faction which drew up the Leaguer declarations of Péronne in 1576. Since Chancellor L'Hospital had asked the clergy to enumerate its property, and since the third estate had demanded at the Estates General of Pontoise in 1561 that the clergy should sell their temporal sources of revenue, the entire French church had felt itself to be under attack, and thenceforth had appealed to the Pope and to Spain for support. This circumstance had a major influence in French history and loosed the storm of civil war upon France. The peace of Monsieur in 1576 was an apparent victory for the Protestants after John Casinir's German invasion. Together with the sale of a part of church property in 1576 and the seizure of the securities guaranteed by the Hôtel de Ville, it threw Parisian democracy and the army of the Church into common revolt. But reference to the act that constituted the League, drawn up in the name of the Most Holy Trinity, makes it perfectly clear that municipal institutions, and, particularly, the local franchises of Paris, counted for nothing in the minds of the organisers of the League. The discovery of the instructions of the advocate David, setting forth the claims of the Guises, proved that their design was pre-eminently a political one, aimed at the crown of France and the abolition of the liberties of the Gallican church. It is difficult to see in the Treaty of Joinville, which was signed on January 16th 1585 between the princes of Lorraine and Spain, anything other than a declaration of war against ideas favouring toleration. The Parisian committees certainly played some part in the treaty, but it was Spain and the Holy See that alone profited from it. The second manifesto of Péronne (March 31st 1585) was animated by the same spirit. It is true that certain vague protests against the enormity of the taxes that overwhelmed the people can be read into it, and yet it was always the nobility that pleaded for its own cause, together with that of the clergy, and insisted upon the preservation of the most aristocratic of privileges. Even more revealing is the fact that when, after the death of Mary Queen of Scots on February 18th 1587, the Parisian masses threatened to transform the character of the League, Mayenne left Paris, and the duc de Guise made known his lively irritation. It was despite the wishes of Guise that the Parisian committees drew up and sent out to the provincial towns the three letters that contained a kind of plan for a federation of municipalities under the direction of the Catholic princes and the patronage of the Parisian Hôtel de Ville.

In the declaration of Nancy in January 1588, the princes implicitly repudiated the democratic tendencies of their Parisian accomplices, for they demanded no more from the king than the publication of the decrees of the Council of Trent and the establishment of the Inquisition in France. It followed that the higher direction of the party continued to take its orders from Rome and remained purely aristocratic and clerical. The day of the barricades represented nothing more than the triumph of Guise. From the point of view of the municipality, its consequences were the arrest of the *Prévôt des Marchands,* Hector de Pereuse, and the irregular election of preselected municipal officers. La Chapelle-Marteau was merely the humble servant of the Guises, both at Paris and Blois. When in the extremity of his despair Henry III decided to disembarrass himself of his haughty rival and to imprison the Parisian deputies, the furious movements which occurred in Paris did assume, it is true, a completely popular character. But who directed and inspired them? In every case it was the monks and the Leaguer *curés.* Men such as Louchart, Bussy-Leclerc and Senault were only supernumeraries who served a purpose. The true heads of the party hastened to call Mayenne to discipline the fearful undulations of the crowd. As soon as he arrived the General Council of the League, the organ of the Parisian democratic movement, was adroitly filled with bishops and members of the Parlement. One of the first cares of the new leader of the League was to assure the Pope that the General Council in Paris would only act on the orders of the Holy See, and that, immediately following the assassination of the King, it was the Hôtel de Ville itself, which, by its letter of August 7th, placed itself at the feet of the Roman Pontiff.

In short, if one wished to describe the character of the struggle of Paris against King Henry III and to define the spirit of the League, one would say that it was a revolt caused partly by the political errors of the King and partly by his financial exactions — that it was a movement inspired by the Holy See, Spain and the clergy, led by the Guises, and using as its instrument the least enlightened part of the people of Paris.

Spain and the League: The Decay of the Supranational Religious Ideal

DE LAMAR JENSEN

De Lamar Jensen began his university studies at Brigham Young University, where he is now Associate Professor of European History. He gained his doctorate at Columbia University in 1957. Specializing in sixteenth-century diplomatic and intellectual history, his research has been conducted largely in French and Spanish sources. He has contributed a volume on Machiavelli to this series. This extract is taken from his book on Bernadino de Mendoza, Philip II's ambassador in France during the revolt of the League. The study of Mendoza's despatches, many of them newly deciphered, has enabled Professor Jensen to trace the fortunes of supranational Catholic idealism in the course of Spanish endeavours to guide the counsels of the League.

THE REVOLUTION that had begun in Paris with the Day of the Barricades spread rapidly through northern and eastern France after the death of Guise. The assassination of the leader and idol of the Catholic party kindled a fanatic and spontaneous demonstration throughout France which fed on hatred of the ignoble "Vilain Herodes" (Anagram composed from "Henri de Valois") and could only be appeased by ultimately devouring the king. News of the events at Blois reached the stunned populace of Paris on Christmas Eve. Shops and markets were closed as the anguished people rushed to the Hôtel de Guise, to the public squares and parks, and to their parish churches to learn more details. Starting with midnight mass at Notre Dame, the Paris preachers bewailed the catastrophe and called down the vengeance of God upon the "wicked Valois race." These fanatical preachers and pamphleteers soon aroused the hatreds and resentment of the Parisian masses and lashed the people to a frenzy. They not only stirred up the emotional sensitivity of the populace and gave the League movement its greatest drive but also provided the intellectual framework which shaped League theory and policy for the next three years. The agitation increased when it was learned that Guise's brother had also been killed. The fury of the Parisians knew no bounds. The royal arms were torn from the churches and all public places, the king was denounced at every pulpit in Paris, and his image was burned in effigy in great all-night processions. On January 31, the emotions of the Parisians were again aroused when the widowed duchesse de Guise was carried to the Hôtel de Soissons with her infant son, born on January 20. The city assumed sponsorship of the child who was christened François-Paris de Lorraine.

More than mass hysteria had gripped the city; there were also organized and quasi-legal measures taken to denounce the Valois king. On January 8, the theological faculty of the Sorbonne formally and solemnly declared Henry guilty of *lèse-majesté* and thenceforth deposed as king of France. The people were freed from their allegiance to him and were authorized to take up arms against him. The Council of the Sixteen,

Reprinted by permission of the author and the publishers from De Lamar Jensen, *Diplomacy and Dogmatism*, pp. 175–182, 222–225 (Cambridge, Mass.: Harvard University Press), Copyright, 1964, by the President and Fellows of Harvard College.

minus La Chapelle-Marteau, Compans, and others who were prisoners of the king, recovered from their shock and promptly seized the full control of government in Paris. They mobilized the armed strength of the city and proceeded to secure the bridges, squares, and other strong places, and to post guards around the houses of the suspicious Politiques. Charenton and Saint-Cloud were garrisoned, artillery was moved into place to reduce the castle of Le Bois de Vincennes to obedience, and the defenses of the Hôtel de Guise were strengthened. With military control of the city ensured, they next held an open assembly where they elected the duke d'Aumale governor of Paris.

In other cities of the realm similar demonstrations took place. The inhabitants of Orléans barricaded the streets and fortified the town with an entire army against a possible attempt of Henry to subdue it by force. The city of Amiens also fortified itself and issued a public declaration against Henry of Valois. In Chartres, Troyes, Bourges, Lyon, Rouen, and many other cities the League openly declared against the king. The executive system of the Paris League was copied in the provincial towns. In Toulouse the Council of the Eighteen controlled all municipal institutions, including the powerful Parlement de Toulouse, and governed the city through its eighteen classes and professions represented in the council. Even the smallest of League towns had its executive committee of eight, or twelve.

League political theory also became more radical in 1589 under the active pens of Boucher, Rose, Launoy, and others. The divine and contractual basis of monarchy were knitted together in a manner giving the people ultimate sanction over kings. The original political contract, Boucher affirmed, was between God, people, and monarch; and, if the king violated the compact with either of the others, the people were absolved from their allegiance to him. Henry III, by his activities of the preceding year-and-a-half culminating in the betrayal at Blois, had severed his pact with both people and God and forfeited his right to rule in France.

On February 15, Mayenne entered Paris amid the wild acclamation of the populace and began to reorganize the League government of France. It was agreed that a central council of government was needed, with powers not only to coordinate the decisions of the various league cities but to serve as a provisional government of France until a new king could be instituted. The great council which emerged on February 17 was chosen from among the Leaguers of Paris and surrounding cities. Four bishops (of Senlis, Meaux, Agen, and Rennes) were among the first members, along with the violent Paris priests of Saint-Benoist (Boucher), Saint-Séverin (Prévost), Saint-André des Arts (Aubry), Saint-Jacques la Boucherie (Pelletier), and Saint-Nicholas des Champs (Pigenat). Some twenty-one lawyers were also represented on the council and the remainder was composed of military officers loyal to Mayenne. This new ruling body of Catholic France, officially titled the *Conseil général de l'Union* but popularly known as the Council of Forty, claimed all the prerogatives and authority of the crown. It assumed the appointment to all state offices and crown benefices, maintained the right of pardon, claimed the power of sending and receiving diplomatic representatives (two envoys were immediately dispatched, one to Philip and one to the pope, to solicit their protection and support with money and men), and demanded the receipt of all royal revenues. The council won immediate popularity in much of France by reducing the amount of taxation and by abolishing the sale and purchase of administrative offices.

One of the first acts of this Council of Forty was to name the duke of Mayenne as lieutenant-general of France, to act as head of the state until a new king was installed. This was to be done by an Estates General which was called to meet in Paris on July 15, to create "a new king and to establish a definitive government." To make the break with the past complete, the new government had a new state seal engraved, obtained a formal declaration from the Sorbonne, and had the edict of sovereignty registered by the Parlement de Paris. With the Paris success, even the Politique Jean Bodin joined the League at Laon and in March took the oath of allegiance to the new union.

The League apparently now governed France, yet Mendoza maintained a cautious attitude in his reporting to Philip. He favoured the declaration of the Union, but he was doubtful about the efficiency of such a large governing body and uncertain of Mayenne's intentions. He was also convinced, as early as February, that Henry of Valois would now attempt a *rapprochement* with Navarre, which could be very damaging to the Catholic cause.

But proclaiming a new government and having it recognized and accepted can be very different things. The new League council, with Mayenne at its head, did not win immediate national and international support. Henry III, just as Mendoza had predicted, began to awake to the peril of his situation and to look around for friends and allies. His first and clumsiest steps were toward a reconciliation with Mayenne and the League nobility. These overtures were rebuffed, however, and Henry angrily issued a declaration against the League. The king turned next to his brother-in-law, Henry of Navarre, and proposed an alliance of the two against the League-dominated north. Navarre was now in a much better bargaining position than he had been in 1586, and was able to win favourable concessions from the French king. Among other things, the Protestants would be permitted to retain all of their previous possessions and conquests; as Navarre advanced northward across the Loire he would be granted a city or fortress in every district (*sénéchaussée*) conquered by him (the rest were to be turned over to Henry); and in all of the cities Navarre should take, even those returned to the French king, the free exercise of the Protestant religion was guaranteed. On 3 April 1589, the alliance, negotiated in behalf of Navarre by Du Plessis-Mornay, was completed.

Mendoza was aroused by the agreement which he considered to be another example of the king's complete unscrupulousness. In letters to Spain the ambassador vigorously denounced Henry, and even wrote to the French king himself, censuring him for joining the heretics in their ignoble campaign against the Christian world. In his informative dispatch of April 26, Mendoza attributed a large share of the responsibility for reconciling the two kings to the activities of the Politiques, who, he felt, were ruining the country and the Church by their selfish personal interests and their lack of religious principles.

On April 30, the alliance was consummated by the meeting of the two kings at Plessis-lès-Tours, where they drew up their plans for the forthcoming campaign. This new alignment was of utmost importance, for it marked a major shift in the tenuous power balance in France. Had it not come about there is a strong likelihood that the League would have gained complete control of the country. It also reveals the increasing political orientation of the opponents to the League. It was really the position and philosophy of the Politiques, not that of the Huguenots, that prevailed at Plessis-lès-Tours and provided the bond between the two kings. The war was rapidly becoming one of religious fanaticism and theocracy versus political reason of state rather than Catholicism versus Protestantism.

Philip II, like the other monarchs of Europe, was not yet ready to recognize the new revolutionary government in Paris as long as the legal ruler, Henry III, was alive and still maintaining himself with a certain amount of power. Philip left no doubt that he would continue to support Mayenne and the League, but officially he still acknowledged Henry as king and refused to sever relations with him. Mendoza remained as Philip's resident ambassador to the French crown and official spokesman at the court of the Most Christian King. Nevertheless, Mendoza's status had been altered considerably since the assassination of Guise. Philip had ordered his ambassador to reject any audience with the king and that order had not been countermanded. For his own part, Henry, who had no love for Mendoza anyway, rebuffed the ambassador with words forceful enough to let him know he was no longer welcome at court. Philip's instructions to Mendoza were to remain close to the king and find out all he could about Henry's intentions, moves, and negotiations, without direct intercourse with the court itself.

In March, when Henry moved from Blois to Tours, Mendoza once more resumed his residence in Paris where he would be in a more favourable position to follow the activities of both Henry and Navarre. But an equally compelling reason for the move was the fast-changing events in Paris itself. The widespread manifestations of the League against Henry III were welcomed by Philip and Mendoza, but they could also become dangerous to the Catholic cause if not properly oriented and led. The new revolutionary Council of the Union, with Mayenne at its head, was as much a question mark to the Spanish king and ambassador as it was to the king of France.

In Mendoza's mind, the most uncertain link in the new union was Mayenne himself, who was a very different person from his brother. Guise had been a strong defender of the universal Catholic ideology in France, and by his death Spain had lost one of the greatest supporters of its crusade to re-establish the *res publica Christiana*. In many ways his death was an irreparable loss to the cause he represented. His ability to lead both the nobility and the masses, his reckless energy and quick decision, and his self-confidence and unscrupulousness were not reproduced in his younger brother. Even the Huguenots — though they could not tolerate the cause he represented — never depreciated Guise's personal courage nor his capacity as a shrewd tactician and a vigorous and skillful military leader. Some who knew him intimately even saw an element of patience and mildness mixed in with Guise's fanaticism.

Mayenne, on the other hand, was no demagogue. He had little feeling for the lower classes and disliked the violence of the mob as well as the "democratic" leanings of the Paris League. He was an honest aristocrat who preferred the company of other aristocrats and refined gentlemen. Where Guise was rash, lavish, and ambitious, Mayenne was cautious, thrifty and conservative. Even their causes were not the same. Guise saw the Holy League as an institution for promoting his personal ambitions; but it was also a means of restoring the religious unity of Europe, and, although he was undoubtedly less idealistic about Christendom than was Philip, he saw no great contradiction nor disloyalty in supporting and being supported by the king of Spain. Outwardly at least, they were both working toward a common goal. Mayenne was not moved by such ideals. His loyalties were confined to France; his enemies were the enemies of France. Mayenne distrusted the more fanatical manifestations of the League as he distrusted the interference of Spain. His only goal was the continued religious orthodoxy of France and the seating of a Catholic prince on the vacant Valois throne. In a very real sense, Mayenne was a Politique himself. The contradiction of this position was his almost complete dependence upon Philip for financial aid. From February on, the League began to move in two different directions.

* * *

Some summary observations about the general nature of the period covered in this study and the particular place occupied in it by Mendoza and the League seem in order. It is only by recognising the importance of religious motivation in the minds of many of the policymakers of the time that the international activity between

Spain and France comes into a consistent focus. Personal, dynastic, economic and political factors all contributed heavily to the course of events in France, but it seems also adequately demonstrated that the religious issue played a leading role, at least in the policies of Philip II and of the League between 1584 and 1591. Philip's costly support of an organisation which in structure and in political theory was the very antithesis of his own beliefs and traditions and which was led by one of the most serious rivals to the house of Hapsburg makes little sense in political and economic terms. In view of the religious goal and duty envisaged by the Catholic King, his actions are more comprehensible. Yet, it is not always easy to distinguish between Philip's Spanish policy and his Catholic policy; to him they appear to have been synonymous.

The turning point in the direction pursued by the League after its refounding in 1584 was the murder of the duke of Guise at the end of 1588. With Guise removed from the helm, the League swerved recklessly from its course. Some segments of it, gathered in and guided by Mendoza and the Paris Sixteen, continued to follow the path marked out by Philip's conception of the Counter Reformation, but an ever-growing body of Leaguers joined with the more nationalistic aims of Mayenne and veered sharply towards the nationalist Gallicanism of the Politiques. Nothing Philip would do could prevent the split. The more actively he participated in the affairs of that kingdom, the more Catholics he alienated. Mendoza's retirement in 1591, the fanaticism of the Sixteen, Parma's death in 1592, the growing nationalistic and anti-Spanish feeling in France, and the effective work of the Politiques and the Parlement de Paris all prepared the way for Navarre's success in 1593.

What did the defeat of the extremists, both Catholic and Protestant, and the victory of the Politiques, mean to France and to the future religious and political development of Europe? First of all, it meant the revival of personal, and soon almost absolute, monarchy in France. Parties and principles gradually gave way to authority and political expediency. Royalism became more popular and fashionable than it had been for many decades. The freshness and spirit of the new Bourbon dynasty won the loyalty of many segments of French society which had felt nothing but contempt for the declining Valois. But some of the methods used by Henry IV to win the fidelity of his subjects created endless difficulties for the future. Much of the immediate loyalty and support he gained was at the expense of long-range control over the nobility and the bureaucracy. His heirs were to feel the real effects of Henry IV's popularity.

In France the triumph of the Politiques meant a victory for the Gallican Church, but, even more important, it revealed the first flicker of light announcing the dawn of a distant day of religious toleration. The beginning of this new attitude toward religion was a victory for the kind of tolerance represented by Montaigne, as characterised in his criticism of the Religious Wars:

> In my time I have seen marvels in the prodigious ease with which people allow themselves to be led by the nose, and made to believe and hope whatever their leaders please. . . . A man is no member of a movement if he dares to breast the wave, if he does not roll in with the tide. As for me, I should have to hate too many people. . . . We have not need to harden our hearts with steel armor; enough if our shoulders are hardened. It will do to dip our pens in ink, without dipping them in blood. Righteousness must be made to prevail over duty.

As for the rest of Europe, the end of the League also began a decline in the supranational religious ideal represented by Philip of Spain. Religious controversies did not cease in 1598 and religious motives in political affairs were prominent for years to come, but the biggest step towards creating a predominantly secular approach to political affairs, especially in international relations, had been made. No one after Philip II ever seriously attempted to recreate the *res publica Christiana* in Europe. England and Germany were still to struggle through their own religious wars, but the solution found in France to the problems unleashed by the Reformation eventually became recognized as the most practical solution for the rest of Europe.

A concluding word about Mendoza himself. The League was not an isolated French institution. It was intricately involved in the international struggle which engaged all of western Europe in the late sixteenth century. Mendoza's connection with it, even while he was accredited ambassador to France, can hardly be overemphasized. Through the various mediums described, Mendoza was able to influence and guide the strategy of the Council of Sixteen, and with it much of the League, in accordance with the desires and plans of the king of Spain. Even more important was Mendoza's friendship and continual communication with the duke of Guise. As a rule, Paris and the other League towns of France adhered rather closely to Guise's orders and leadership, while he in turn—in spite of strong personal ambitions—did what he was instructed from Spain. Few of the major League decisions or operations between 1584 and December 1588 were undertaken without direct orders from Philip, or at least without complete Spanish knowledge and approval. After the death of Guise, Mendoza's role in the activities of the League, and especially of the Sixteen, was even more intimate. Many times decisions were made and tactics planned under his leadership and advice. When Henry III was removed from the scene in 1589, Mendoza became an official agent to the League, with instructions to advise, influence, and even direct its activity and planning. In the meantime, the split which occurred within the League reduced the extent of Mendoza's influence, although within its smaller orbit he seems to have been stronger than before. On the other hand, the wing of the League led by Mayenne disliked him almost as much as they did Navarre and the Huguenots.

Noble Faction and Republican Independence: Provence and Marseille

FERNAND BRAUDEL

M. Braudel was born at Lunéville (Meuse) in 1902. In the early part of his career he taught at such celebrated schools as the *lycée Condorcet* and the *lycée Henry IV*. Receiving a doctorate of letters in 1947, he also holds honorary doctorates from the universities of Sao Paulo, Brussels, Oxford, Geneva and Madrid. He is Director of Studies and President of the Sixth Section of the *Ecole pratique des hautes etudes*, Professor of the History of Modern Civilization at the *Collège de France* and Director of the review, *Annales-Economies, Sociétés, Civilisations.* His magnificent study of late sixteenth-century Mediterranean civilization based upon economic and geographic considerations, from which the following extract is taken, has won universal acclaim.

IN PROVENCE the struggle had begun before the death of Henry III. It lasted much longer than in neighboring Languedoc, and in its repercussions it was prolonged until the end of the Franco-Spanish War in 1598 (the date of the evacuation of Berre by its small Savoyard garrison).

As early as April 1589 Provence had seceded, or, more precisely, the Parlement of Aix had adhered to the Catholic League and recognised the duc de Mayenne as "Lieutenant-General of the Kingdom." In July of the same year a feeble "royalist" minority from the Parlement had withdrawn to Pertuis. The great towns, Aix and Arles and also Marseille (though it was outside Provence while being in the same geographic area) were all in favour of the League. This meant that the whole provençal area, dominated by its bourgeois towns sheltering behind their privileges, had taken its stand even before the advent of the new King of France. The duc d'Epernon, appointed governor in 1587, had resigned in favour of his brother, Bernard de Nogaret de Lavalette. The latter was active and energetic and did not abandon hope in face of the new danger. He was faithful to the royal government and would rely upon the forces of the royalist Lesdiguières in Dauphiné and upon the popular and peasant classes. He stood firm against disorder and even succeeded in reoccupying central and southern Provence. A Spanish report of 1590 revealed that he was fortifying Toulon against Savoy, as well as against all the dangers that might come from the Mediterranean coast. Yet Lavalette could not impose his will upon Provence with any greater success than the others who, in one sense or another, tried to do so in the last ten terrible years of the struggle. In fact until 1596 there were always at least two Provences, hostile to one another and with fluctuating, indeterminate frontiers between them. One was attached to Aix, and the other to the provisional royalist capital of Pertuis.

Marseille, by far the most important single factor in the area, had joined the cause of the League after the assassination of the second royalist consul, Lenche, in April 1588, and had rallied again to the cause

From Fernand Braudel, *La Méditerranée et le Monde méditerranéen à l'époque de Philippe II* (Paris, 1949), pp 1059–1067. Reprinted by permission of the author. [Editor's translation.]

with a passion that was beyond contradiction. To come to an understanding with the League implied, sooner or later, to join in association with Spain.

However, in the summer of 1590 the only foreign intrigue that appeared to be developing in Provence was that of Savoy. Savoy was very much a minor partner, but it was well placed to act, and far more able to disturb Provence than the mighty and far-off ruler of Spain. In answer to the call of a feminine leader of the League with a penchant for intrigue, Christine Daguerre, comtesse de Sault, Charles Emmanuel of Savoy invaded Provence in July. On November 17th 1590 he arrived at Aix, where the Parlement received him, and entrusted him with the provincial military government — but without granting him the status of Count of Provence, the real object of his ambitions.

All the elements in the provençal drama were assembled on the stage in the winter of 1590. If the action was slow to develop, this was because Spain, appreciating that Savoy could no more impose a single authority in Provence than herself, preferred to intervene first in Languedoc. After the crisis in Aragon in 1592 and the disastrous defeat of Villemur, the secondary theatre of Provence became the only possible area for the extension of Spanish influence in Mediterranean France, and the Spanish then intervened in the area with a vigour they had never shown before. Yet they did not move with such speed or haste that they pushed such local actors as Savoy, Lesdiguières and Lavalette off the stage.

The winter campaigns of Lesdiguières late in 1591 and early in 1592 revealed the weakness of the Duke of Savoy. In cooperation with Lavalette Lesdiguières threw back the Savoyard forces beyond the River Var, and, after Lavalette's death on January 11th 1592 from a wound received in the siege of Roquebrune, he advanced in the spring to surprise the Duke on his own territory in Niçois. Although the Savoyard garrisons scattered throughout Provence were blockaded rather than besieged, their anxiety was far from inconsiderable. But Lesdiguières returned to the Alps, and in the summer the forces of Savoy were permitted to make a new promenade through Provence, capturing Cannes and Antibes in August 1592. These successes could be no more decisive than the preceding ones. The war extended over a ruined countryside and was reduced to a series of sudden surprise attacks where the victor celebrated empty triumphs. At the death of his brother the duc d'Epernon took over his governorship and installed himself with his troop of Gascon adventurers as though in a conquered country. Towards autumn a series of direct blows and energetic moves, marked by atrocious cruelties, enabled him to retake Cannes and Antibes from Savoy. Affairs seemed to be moving in a new direction. As early as September the representatives of "anti-royalist" Provence turned to the King of Spain to ask his aid. The comte de Carcès, who had been named the Leaguer governor of Provence by his father-in-law, Mayenne, in 1592, renewed this request early in 1593. But these alarms were unnecessary. In June and July 1593 the duc d'Epernon failed to take the town of Aix, and it seemed that the complete success that had twice been refused to Savoy was denied him also.

At this very point the King's abjuration of Protestantism changed the complexion of events in France as a whole. A vast movement of rallying to the crown followed, a passionate devotion to the person of the King and the ideal of peace. On January 5th 1594 the Parlement of Aix took an oath of loyalty to the King. It was the first of the Leaguer Parlements to recognise Henry IV, but, though this seemed a decisive act at the time, it was not to prove so. In Provence that year did indeed prove to be one of realignment and renunciation but it was also filled with the final series of intrigues and revolts, with false calculations, violent deeds and a thousand plots and corruptions — in all a dust cloud containing a myriad of particles of individual actions.

There was, however, one element of great significance that did emerge at this time. The Leaguer factions that were turning towards Henry IV drew closer together and directed all their bitterness against Epernon. The latter's intent then became clear. He knew that he was not liked by the King, for he had brought pressure upon him to grant the government of Provence in 1592. He was deeply hated by the Provençal nobility, and he realised that the prospect of peace spelt the end of his authority and the ruin of his hopes to establish an independent principality. The future seemed black for him, and he had good reason not to desire an understanding with the people of Aix and the nobility. Nor was it surprising that he felt concern at the activities of that remarkable diplomatic agent whom Henry IV had sent into the midst of the provençal intrigues, Jacques de Beauvais La Fin. However, when Lesdiguières and Montmorency intervened, he was obliged to follow the King's instructions to come to terms with Aix. Then the bad faith of Lesdiguières, and the announcement that the son of Henri de Guise was to be governor of Provence, determined Epernon to revolt, in order to preserve, as he put it, his honour and his life. Revolt necessarily implied an understanding with Spain and Savoy. According to his own letters and to Spanish sources, he had taken this step as early as November 1594. It was not until a year later, however, that a clear agreement made his treason unequivocal. The Duke went over to the enemy with his Gascons, the few towns he still held in Provence, and even, so it seems, some outside Provence. The Spanish archives contain an interesting list of the properties and towns throughout France which the duc d'Epernon claimed to possess.

Yet Epernon's treason had been too long delayed. When the alliance with Spain was finally drawn up in due form in November 1595, the fate of the south had already been decided. Nevertheless it is too easily forgotten that in 1594 Spain had decided to make a great effort. Velasco, the Constable of Castile and Governor of Milan, had assembled a considerable army and was prepared to launch an offensive with it beyond Savoy and the Jura Mountains towards Dijon. Marshal de Rosne even advised him to establish his base at Moulins in Bourbonnais on the "Ailly" [Allier] in order to maintain his cavalry. In that summer of 1595 the very heart of France was threatened. On June 5th the victory of Fontaine Française determined the repulse of the invasion. Although the engagement was insignificant enough from a military point of view, it had important consequences. Henry IV's march to the south had left the north unprotected; but it had consolidated positions, stretching as far as the Mediterranean coast, that would have compromised the wide turning movement planned by his adversary.

In 1596 order was restored throughout Provence and both Epernon and the town of Marseille were brought under control. The duc de Guise had little difficulty in quelling these two last obstacles to peace. In February the "royalist" forces severely handled Epernon's small army at Vidauban. The fighting continued even in the waters of the Argens River, where many men were drowned. On 26th March Epernon made his peace with the King, and left Provence two months later. Meanwhile treachery within Marseille had opened the city gates to the duc de Guise on the night of February 16th–17th.

As in many of the towns of France in these troubled years [1588–1596] Marseille regained its autonomy. Independent, Catholic and Leaguer, it surrendered itself to the passions aroused from April 1588. But how was it possible to exist on the extremity of the kingdom? In actual fact it was excluded from a country whose troubled state had brought economic chaos. In this respect the requests made to Spain for grain supplies tell their story. On the other hand, the war that encircled the town from far and near was not a modern war: it was a battle of men rather than of resources.

Even so, it proved a costly battle. The town watch had to be maintained at Marseille, and contributions to military expenses were exacted. A policy arousing strong convictions was needed to secure consent to sacrifices. For five years such a policy was incarnated in the person of Charles de Casaulx whose actions have been freshly and clearly illuminated, though not justified at any price, by his most recent historian, Raoul Busquet. This energetic leader of men seized the seat of municipal government in February 1591 in true revolutionary fashion. He served as a watchful and effective administrator of the city's affairs. His single loyalty to this task provided a policy that immediately proved itself independent of the threatening intrigues of the Duke of Savoy, who desired to use Marseille as a means of direct liaison with Spain. In March 1591 the Duke's visit to the city proved a vain one, and his attempt to seize the city by the treachery of Saint-Victor (November 16th and 17th 1591) was doomed to similar disappointment. Casaulx kept firmly apart from the quarrels and intrigues of the Provençal nobility, and although Marseille served briefly as a place of refuge for the Countess de Saulx, the dictator cleverly secured her removal.

A little reflection on the popular policy of Casaulx in Marseille, especially on what might be called his work of public assistance, with his careful introduction of the printing works and his programme of building, may reveal his so-called "tyranny" in a new light. Certainly, as with any tyranny, police-state methods were used against his enemies, the *bigarrats,* who were unhesitatingly imprisoned, exiled and deprived of their goods. Yet the régime was popular, and, oddly enough, in the interests of the mass of the poor. A Spanish report shows that in 1594 a campaign was launched against the rich merchants or noblemen. "It is difficult to know the reason for this," stated the report, "but doubtless it is means of obtaining money from them." As mistress of its own destiny, the city may have seemed likely to have been overwhelmed by the heavy burden it bore. When the Pope and the Grand Duke of Tuscany were asked to provide aid in 1594, they were not prepared to contribute one silver coin. Sheer necessity, as much as his own ideology, obliged Casaulx to turn to the power of Spain to win grace and favour, and the means to exist.

In the circumstances the town entered gradually into the sphere of Spanish politics, and eventually became completely involved. On November 16th 1595 the Viguier and the Consuls of Marseille wrote to Philip II a singular letter which, while it still showed prudent reserve in some aspects, was, nevertheless, categorical enough. It is worth pausing for a moment to consider this letter.

"God having inspired in our souls," it declared,

> the sacred fire of His zeal for the maintenance of His cause in this great and perilous shipwreck of the Catholic religion in France, we, standing firm against the shocks that the enemy of the faith and of this estate has tried to inflict upon us, and knowing that, by the particular favour of Heaven, the religion and estate of our city have been so far preserved safe and entire, declare our invincible will to keep it so at the cost of our lives and of those of all our citizens, who are united in constancy through this holy resolution. But foreseeing the rising of the storm through the prosperity of the affairs of Henry de Bourbon and perceiving that neither the public means, which are already exhausted, nor the strength of private individuals, can suffice any longer for the pursuit of this great and salutary enterprise, we have dared to lift our eyes towards Your Catholic Majesty and to have recourse to you . . . as a refuge for all Catholics, begging you humbly to cast the rays of your natural sweetness on a city that deserves so much merit for its ancient religion and faithfulness. . . .

It should be noted that, at least according to this document, Marseille did not surrender itself to the King of Spain. There are relative degrees in its "treason." The city (or rather Casaulx) declared only that it would never withdraw from the struggle.

A fairly lengthy anonymous propaganda pamphlet said precisely this when it was printed late in 1595 or early in 1596. This diffuse piece was entitled *The Reply of the French Catholics and Town of Marseille to the Advice of Their Heretical, Politique, Antichristian and Atheistical Neighbours.* It added little that was new to the paper controversies that accompanied the Wars of Religion. It made no attempt at objectivity, describing royalists as atheists and Huguenots as given to wanton immorality. It was a facile little polemic, and its violence and virulence appear somewhat unsavoury in perspective. The only thing to notice is that it said not one word about the town's relations with Spain.

Nevertheless, this agreement brought inescapable consequences: it was necessary to shelter behind the vast power of Spain, and to come to an understanding with the royal agent, President Etienne Bernard, who established himself in Marseille and made dazzling promises to Casaulx and his henchman, Louis d'Aix. There might have been some suspicion that these promises were a little too lavish. Might they not have concealed a trap? The masters of Marseille preferred to deal directly with Philip II. Three "deputies" of the city, one of whom was a son of Casaulx himself, made the journey to Spain. This was an opportunity for them to draw up a long account of the events in Marseille from 1591 to 1595 and to set out the role of the "dictators," Louis d'Aix and Casaulx, who, as sons of old Marseille families, had been able to use the support of their relatives, their friends and the city populace to create Catholic peace and order. [Their success was not achieved without difficulties.] They had to arm, to raise mercenaries, to occupy the fortress of Notre-dame, Saint-Victor and the Saint-Jehan tower, to guard the Reale gate, the great platform and the Aix gate — the strong points in the defences — to build Fort Christien at the mouth of the harbour (though this was not completed), to keep horses to secure the surrounding lands and permit the people of Marseille to gather their crops without interference from the enemy. When Henri de Bourbon had been absolved by the Pope and triumphed over his opponents, when he had become master of the town of Arles, which was then a means of replenishing the city's grain supplies, and Marseille had become full of refugees, including that "great and learned personage Monseigneur de Gembrard [Génébrard] Archbishop of Aix, dispossessed by Henri de Bourbon," then, in such extremities and despite the offers of the Béarnais, the city could only survive "under the wing" of the Catholic King of Spain. He alone could offer aid, and offer it quickly, in the form of money, munitions, men and galleys. The situation became even more critical when the royal troops advanced to the gates of Marseille and when plots were hatched within the city walls.

In December 1595 help arrived at Marseille in the form of the galleys of Prince Doria's son and two Spanish companies, just in time to prevent the entry of the royal troops. But within Marseille the situation became confused and disturbing: its citizens began to turn even against their own friends. On January 21st 1596 the Marseille deputies left the Spanish court having achieved their purpose. The city surrendered itself to the Catholic King in fact but not in theory. Philip II had free access to the port for his galleys, the possibility of installing troops, and the promise of the Marseillais not to treat with Henri de Béarn and not to recognise anyone save a friend of Spain as King of France. The people of Marseille, stated the *mémoire* of the deputies,

> will not recognise Henri de Bourbon, nor will they adhere to any other enemies of Your Catholic Majesty, and thus they will maintain and preserve themselves as Catholics in their present state until it may please God to give France a Christian and truly Catholic king who may be in good friendship, brotherhood and intimacy with Your Catholic Majesty.

On February 12th, 1596 the deputies were still at Barcelona, whence they wrote to Don Juan de Idiaquez to ask him for Catalan wheat. But four days later, on the 17th, a conspiracy succeeded in the city. Casaulx had been assassinated and the town delivered to Henry IV. "And now I am really King of France," declared the latter when he received the good news.

It would be possible to write at greater length on that fragment of French history presented by events in Provence under the League. Reputable historians would tell us that we should find there all the characteristics of the last years of our wars of religion — the price rise, the terrible poverty in town and countryside, the leprous growth of brigandage and the blind fury of the politics of the nobility. One might study Epernon as an example of the so-called "kings" of the French provinces, such as Lesdiguières (a man of very different character yet with the same role) in Dauphiné, or Mercoeur in Brittany, or Mayenne in Burgundy. It would be still more tempting to see in the example of Marseille the overwhelming importance of the towns first in the dislocation and then in the reconstruction of France.

The League was not just an alliance of fervent Catholics, nor was it merely an instrument at the disposal of the Guises. It was also a rolling back of the processes of time, a return to the advantages of past conditions which the monarchy had opposed and then partially suppressed. In particular, it was a return to the independent urban life of the city-state. The advocate Le Breton, hanged in November 1586, was doubtless a little mad, but all the same it is significant that one can find in his plans a return to urban franchises, a dream-like project of breaking up the country into little Catholic republics, each of them mistress of its own destiny. The treason of the towns proved to be as serious as that of the Guises — a treason by entire populations carried away by their convictions, from their bourgeois to the most humble of their artisans. Paris was the greater model for these towns. In 1595 the Duke de Feria proposed to Archduke Albert that he should attempt to reconstruct a League in France on the same principles as those of the time of Henry III,

> which League was not founded by the princes of the house of Lorraine, but by several bourgeois of Paris and other towns, only three or four of them in the beginning. . . . under such Christian and well-advised conditions that the major and best part of France would join them.

Some of these men were still in Brussels. The mistakes and betrayal of the leaders had certainly not resulted in the entire defeat of the cause.

This underlines to the point of exaggeration the decisive role of the towns. But were they able to survive for long in independent revolt? The rupture of communications meant the ruin of trade and ultimately the suicide of the towns. If after 1593 they rallied willingly to the victory of Henry IV it is surely not just for the reasons normally advanced to explain their attitude, but rather because they could not live in isolation — because they needed the larger economic environment to survive. If there was such a need, then Marseille, incapable of living from the sea alone without the aid of the hinterland and the connexion with France, shows us the indispensable symbiosis of the land and sea routes in the whole Mediterranean area.

III. CONSEQUENCES

The Development of Political Ideas

J. H. M. SALMON

J. H. M. Salmon is a graduate of the universities of Cambridge and New Zealand. He held the foundation chair of History at the University of New South Wales (Sydney) before becoming Professor of History and Dean of Humanities at the University of Waikato (Hamilton, New Zealand). In this first of five selections on the consequences of the French Wars of Religion, Professor Salmon discusses the Wars' effect on the growth of modern political concepts.

However diverse the social and economic causes now assigned to the dissensions experienced in various European states in the sixteenth and seventeenth centuries, contemporary explanation of politics was generally attempted in terms of religious belief. It was in France that the political effects of the Reformation first stimulated a radical examination of European traditions which resulted in the transformation of European political theory. The French Religious Wars were the first demonstration of these effects within a sovereign state. This was not evident in the earlier Schmalkaldic Wars in Germany, because the constitution of the Empire made these less a civil war than a conflict between virtually sovereign princes. The solution of *cuius regio eius religio* sustained this view, and the Thirty Years War confirmed it. Nor did the initiative in the transformation of European thought arise from the Revolt of the Netherlands, which, though it was contemporary with the French conflicts and in some phases inseparable from them, was largely dependent upon French political theory. Theory and event in Scotland followed similarly in the wake of those in France.

Thus it was the French conflicts which provided the initial stimulus to the enunciation of modern political concepts. It was French thought which first essayed the task of adapting medieval controversies between a universal church and a supposedly universal state to the political and religious problems of a modern nation state.

* * *

No one who has followed the political vagaries of the French Wars of Religion can fail to remark the curious way in which the events dictated the development of ideas. Huguenot theories of resistance went through three distinct phases until the death of the youngest son of Catherine de' Medici made the Protestant Henri of Navarre the heir to the Valois crown, and caused his following to espouse the principles of hereditary absolute monarchy. It was then the turn of the Catholic Ligue, opposing the Bourbon succession, to repeat the phases of Huguenot resistance theory. Under the weight of this new assault, an assault sanctified by Papal blessing, the Politique monarchical writers changed the emphasis in their thought from the legalist view of sovereignty to that theory of Divine

From J. H. M. Salmon, *The French Religious Wars in English Political Thought* (Oxford, 1959), pp. 4–11, 13–14. Reprinted by permission of the Clarendon Press.

Right which James I imported into England to fire the long train of seventeenth century conflicts.

The first phase of Huguenot opposition was directed against the king's advisers, and not against the person or status of the monarch. It clung to the principle of legitimacy in its insistence upon the leadership of its own movement by the princes of the blood. After what appeared to be a flagrant betrayal of trust by the monarchy in the origins of the third civil war in 1568, it turned to a kind of historical constitutionalism, which sought for precedents to support those who claimed the role of guardians of an ancient constitution. Inevitably such a theme became a theory of limited monarchy, though the limitations were seldom precise and were usually advanced in terms of immemorial custom. It made use of moderate opinions such as those expressed by Claude de Seyssel in the age preceding the exaltation of absolute monarchy by the *légistes* of the reigns of François I and Henri II.

The enormity of the act of St. Bartholomew's night called forth a new response from Huguenot theorists. They appealed to reason rather than to history. At the same time they continued to employ their constitutional myths of the power of the Estates General, and to quote historical precedents to disguise revolutionary action as conservatism. They returned to the anarchic conflicts of Armagnacs and Burgundians. They explored remoter ages to prove the constitutional deposition of the Merovingian and Carolingian dynasties. But behind this façade of historical experience they proceeded on *a priori* grounds to construct general propositions about the nature and organisation of political society. They wove rational arguments to show that the community in its corporate capacity possessed an ultimate sovereignty which enabled its representatives to discipline or depose the ruler. Even François Hotman in his *Franca-Gallia* selected and twisted the historical facts to serve the needs of Huguenot logic. The argument that French kings had been elected and deposed by their people until comparatively recent times was intended to show that the ruler was still *virtually* elected and might be deposed by his subjects. This conclusion would not follow from the historical argument, and it can therefore be taken that history was quoted as empirical verification of an *a priori* set of assumptions. For Hotman it was in the nature of the descendants of the Francogauls, and hence in their institutions, that there should be means of dealing with a tyrant.

The main *rex singulis major, universis minor* epitomized the theory of popular sovereignty as it was expressed in the *Vindiciae contra Tyrannos* and the writings of Beza after the massacre. Its reasoning was derived from Aristotelian premises which described a human society as alone providing a full life for its members, and which endowed such a society with an organic unity. The ruler existed to promote the welfare of the whole society. If he placed his own welfare before the collective good of his subjects, he no longer fulfilled his function. The society as a whole was greater than he, and those who represented it might take action against him. Arguments of this kind had been implicit in medieval thought. They had been advanced on behalf of the temporal ruler against the Papacy to show that the emperor or king had received his power from God through the mediation of his people and not through that of the Pope. They had been employed in the Conciliar Controversy to show that the Council of the Church represented a communal power greater than that of its earthly head.

These lines of reasoning had been popular in France among Gallican churchmen and secular opponents of the Papal *plenitudo potestatis* since the thirteenth century, but they had never been applied to a situation where open rebellion against the monarchy took place within what was at last realised to be a national society. John Major had expounded the doctrine of the subordination of the king to the will of the whole community two generations before, but then the Roman precedents of universalism had obscured its radical implications. Now the doctrine of popular sovereignty lost its scholastic context, and emerged from the chrysalis of academic controversy to spread its wings as the slogan of popular revolt. In the hands of French theorists of resistance the concept became a revolutionary force because within a national society it was no longer the latent sanction for the existence of authority, but an active incitement to overturn it. Roman Law controversies over an original transference of power from people to ruler, either conditionally or irrevocably, were adapted to the new situation. Theories of contract became an essential part of the doctrine of popular sovereignty. It was assumed that such sovereignty would be exercised by the natural leaders of society. There was no conscious attempt to express this in the pseudo-rational terms of a *volonté générale*. For this it was necessary to await the age when the common man would rebel against his traditional masters.

Many Huguenot writers were aware of the fact that there was nothing specifically Calvinist about these secular opinions. Some, who expounded them in terms of contracts between King and people, added contracts between God and people, so that resistance might become a spiritual duty. Others asserted that these views were consistent with the penultimate paragraph in Calvin's *Institutes* where it was declared that certain "inferior magistrates" might be appointed to safeguard the constitution and in cases of extreme tyranny to resist the ruler. But this was foreign to Calvin's usual emphasis on non-resistance, and in any case it had more in common with the constitutional phase of Huguenot thinking.

The manner in which Huguenot thought became increasingly radical in response to political events was no more remarkable than the comparable reactions of the theorists of the Ligue. When Henri III showed himself more of a Politique than a Catholic in coming to terms with the Huguenots in 1576, the early manifestos of the Ligue showed the same loyalty to the King and the same abhorrence for the policy of his advisers as the Huguenot conspirators had shown at Amboise in 1560. When a heretic became heir to the Valois throne in 1584, and the King seemed likely to accord him recognition, the publicists of the Ligue favoured doctrines of limitation of royal power, and wrote of imprescriptible fundamental laws of the constitution in a way similar to the trend of Huguenot thinking in 1568. The murder of Henri de Guise by the royal command in 1588 produced a response like that which in Protestant propaganda had been inspired by the Massacre of St. Bartholomew. After the assassination of the last Valois in the following year, the Ligue continued to oppose Henry IV with theories of popular sovereignty in uneasy combination with ultramontane views of the Papal power to depose princes and sanction the rebellion of their subjects.

If anything, Ligueur opinions were more radical and extreme than those of their Huguenot predecessors. They promoted the murder of Henri III and justified an attempt upon the life of his successor. The Ligue contained elements of the lower classes which were able for a time to wrest control of Paris from their aristocratic leaders. The ideas which accompanied the reign of *Les Seize* in the capital sometimes anticipated those of a greater revolution two centuries later. On the other hand, the more orthodox Ligueur theorists, such as Rossaeus and Jean Boucher, were able to express the concept of popular sovereignty with greater clarity than their Huguenot counterparts. They felt themselves to be more directly in line with their medieval predecessors, and they did not experience the difficulty of Huguenot writers who strove to reconcile Calvinist federalism with the corporate unity implied in their theory. When they wrote of the corporate action of the whole community, they were closer to reality than those Protestant theorists who had spoken in the name of a mere fraction of French society. Circumstances also forced the Ligue towards a greater understanding of the inherent conflict between the idea of customary law and that of legislative sovereignty. The problem arose very clearly in the debate in the 1593 Estates General to choose a Ligueur candidate for the throne. The sanctity of the Salic Law was defended by the Parlement as the product of immemorial custom, but the Estates showed themselves ready to enact a "fundamental" law concerning the religious orthodoxy of the king.

Thus the fortuitous course of political circumstance drove the theorists of resistance from a conservative dependence upon the past to radical analyses of the nature of political authority in logical rather than historical terms. And, as if to re-emphasize the subjection of theory to event and to reaffirm secular motives concealed beneath religious dogmas, the transformation of Protestant theories was repeated in the process of Catholic opposition to the crown. In reaction to these developments the French proponents of monarchical absolutism were no less radical, for they reposed an irresponsible sovereignty in the ruler alone, and suggested that even the restraint imposed by Natural Law could not be enforced by human agency. Although absolutist theory came increasingly to rely upon the obscurantism of Divine Right, it never lost the logical, juristic definition of legislative sovereignty achieved by Jean Bodin.

. . . The origins of that Age of Enlightenment which established the criteria of modern liberalism are to be sought in the French Wars of Religion, and are to be seen reflected in subsequent English thought. These criteria may be found in the destruction of medieval ideas of custom before the logic of legislative sovereignty, in the transformation of the scholastic concept of Natural Law, or in the new individualist ethic inspired by Protestant theology. These are not disparate strands, but merely ways of differentiating the habits of political thought which we choose to term modern from those we describe as medieval.

Social Disruption and the Undermining of Monarchical Government

JEAN-HIPPOLYTE MARIÉJOL

Jean-Hippolyte Mariéjol (1885–1934) was a professor in the Faculty of Letters at the University of Lyon. He was the author of well-known biographies of Catherine de Medici and her daughter, Marguerite, as well as of the volumes covering the period 1559–1643 in Ernest Lavisse's *History of France,* from which the following extract is taken. Mariéjol combines literary insight with a command of the published sources for the Wars of Religion. This extract gives a general account of the political and social consequences of the wars in preparation for the author's survey of the later achievements of Henry IV.

THE RELIGIOUS WARS had been general wars, party against party, town against town, château against château. The normally pacific sections of the population, bourgeois, workers and even peasants had been combatants. The cost in human lives had been enormous. Destruction had been multiplied by sieges, the passage of armies, burnings, sackings and pillage. A royal declaration of March 16th 1595 stated that farms, parishes and villages were abandoned and depopulated. Tillage had nearly everywhere come to a stop. Public and private resources had dried up or been drastically reduced. The roads had fallen into disrepair; bridges were insecure or collapsed; the banks and walls of water-ways were broken. The King no longer possessed a single royal vessel and the seas were abandoned to pirates of all nationalities. By land and sea merchants were confronted by appalling risks. "France and I," wrote Henry IV on 1st May 1958, "need to pause and draw breath."

In their various ways the three orders of society had suffered severely. The Church had unwittingly contributed to the expenses of the struggle, and in the diocese of Auxerre the clergy in 1593 reckoned the general total at three million livres a year. On this estimate the Church, whose landed property was said by the third estate in 1561 to be worth 120 million livres and to bring in four million livres in annual revenue, must have lost three quarters of its wealth between the two dates. This is clearly an exaggeration, but the sacrifice must have been great.

Unlike the clergy, the nobility had no other sources of revenue with which to make good its losses. The exploitation of the mines of America had provided the Spanish and, through their agency, the other nations of Europe, with a vast quantity of gold and silver, which by its very abundance had caused inflation. According to La Noue the purchasing power of money had fallen to a quarter of its former worth. Seigneurs who had exchanged their land with their peasantry for dues in cash continued to receive the same revenue but no longer the same value. What had cost five sous in the past cost twenty in the time of Henry III. The nobility became impoverished without realizing what was happening.

Yet they had still to go on campaign, to pay their soldiery, to maintain their châ-

From J.-H. Mariéjol, *Histoire de France* (ed. Lavisse) (Paris, 1911), Vol. VI, Part 2; pp. 1–8, 11–14, 18–22. Reprinted by permission of Presses Universitaires de France. [Editor's translation.]

teaux and to protect their lands. La Noue estimated that eighty per cent of the nobility were embarrassed by "alienation of some part of their property, by commitments and other debts." The conflict had entered its fiercest phase after 1585. To aid the indebted gentry the government took a step amounting to social relief by revising contracts of debt. — It remitted the payment of twenty months' interest in every five years. It is true that the same edict required debtors to pay during 1595 and 1596 all remaining arrears as well as current interest under pain of bankruptcy and the refusal of further relief. Yet when in April 1595 the King recalled the nobility to the army with the declaration of war against Spain, he prolonged the period granted for the repayment of debts by three years. The government itself could not pay the interest on the bonds issued through the Paris municipality at this time. The extension of time allowed the indebted nobility did not prove adequate. In July 1601 Henry IV declared that condemnations for debt had been the ruin of several "good and ancient families" and if the evil practice became extended it might well "in the end cause some disturbances in the form of this monarchy comparable to the changes which large debts and the practice of usury have occasioned in the past in a number of commonwealths."

. . . Yet it remained necessary for the indebted class to continue to borrow. Since money was difficult to obtain, and interest charges were heavy, debts could only be discharged ultimately by the surrender or sale of châteaux, houses, fields and seigneuries. Hence during and after the civil wars a vast amount of property changed hands. In 1605 François Miron, the mayor of Paris, estimated that half the land in the kingdom had been sold through the court of the Châtelet. This property, of which the nobility had been the largest owners, passed to those who had kept out of trouble or even had profited from the wars — royal officials, financiers and social upstarts. As early as the beginning of the seventeenth century, wrote Pierre de Vaissière, "in Champagne and near Châteu-Thierry châteaux, fiefs and subfiefs were in the possession of seigneurs and squires whose ancestors had sold cloth in small towns."

If after the peace the nobility of the sword had resigned themselves to living in the country as they had formerly done, they would have been able through the practice of economy to reconstitute and preserve their patrimony. But the nobility had acquired a taste for a different kind of life. For forty years they had been almost continually in arms, fighting for the King, for the Protestant cause or for the League. They had lost the habit of living in the country. They had passed through foreign lands, come into close contact with princes, and experienced the refined luxury and culture of the Valois court. Experience had taught them that service at court was best appreciated, and that service at a distance from the court went unrewarded. They had compared the constant round of festivities at the royal palaces with the gloomy isolation of their châteaux. They were not to forget this experience. Impoverished and demoralised, they sought military and civil offices in the royal household. They abandoned the supervision of their lands for the royal entourage. They ceased to be rural nobility and became, instead, professional courtiers.

Meanwhile, the seigneurs put pressure on the peasantry to provide for new kinds of expenditure and to repair the losses caused by the wars. Pillaged by their friends and their enemies, the peasants could endure their burden no longer and, in their despair, turned to revolt. In 1579–1580 the peasants of Dauphiné, both Protestant and Catholic, took up arms and refused to pay taxes to church and state, and dues to their seigneurs. In 1590 a peasant rising of the *Gauthiers* occurred in Normandy. In 1592 the peasantry near Comminges made a league which they "called *Campanelle* to attack and overwhelm the nobility." In 1594 the peasants of Périgord and Limousin, known as the *Croquants* or

Tard-Avisés took up arms against the nobility. . . . These insurrections were a superficial manifestation of an underlying hostility between seigneur and peasant.

The bourgeois lived on their savings but even their savings wasted away. The government paid the wages of officials in an irregular way and after 1585 the payments of interest on the public debt were so seldom honoured that by 1605 they were sixty million livres in arrears. It had become the custom to seek security in state loans and such investment was made with the capital of widows, minors, marriage portions and bequests to hospitals and charitable institutions. Consequently the suspension of the arrears of debt caused widespread distress.

. . . In the towns unemployed workers, and peasants driven from the fields by insecurity and poverty, formed a multitude of starving beggars. On March 4th 1596 7,769 destitute people were counted in the cemetery of the Innocents in Paris. The towns gave employment as best they could. At Montdidier beggars were enlisted in three companies, each of fifty men, and obliged to work on the fortifications under threats of whipping or banishment. The hospitals were obliged to discharge the sick and ailing, who died for lack of care. From January 1st to February 10th 1596 416 persons died at the Hôtel-Dieu in Paris, mostly from hunger.

The plague was almost endemic within these unfortunate segments of society. 8000 people were carried off at Abbeville within fifteen months (1596–1597), and in 1599 the plague killed 12,000 persons in and about the town. An epidemic of pestilent fevers raged in Paris at the same time, and in 1606 and 1607 these were followed by the plague. So many disasters terrified the imaginations of men, and led many to see in their affliction the signs of divine wrath. "When the war between men was over," wrote the diarist L'Estoile in June 1598, "a war began between wolves and men. Many cruel forays were made by the said wolves, especially in Brie, Champagne and Bassigni." Pasquier did not exaggerate when he wrote that a man who had been asleep for forty years would awake to see "not France, but the corpse of France."

. . . The government had very feeble means at its disposal to deal with all these disorders. The council which the Valois kings had bequeathed to Henry IV was composed of too many men, and men of too high a rank, for the King to be well served. The provincial governors, chosen from the great aristocracy, had extremely wide powers as royal representatives, and during the civil wars they had arrogated to themselves other powers forbidden them in royal ordinances. . . . They were accustomed to consider their offices as hereditary. . . . The parlements remembered the great role they had played in the time of the League. Four out of seven of these parlements (Paris, Toulouse, Aix-en-Provence and Dijon) had not acknowledged the King until after his abjuration. The Leaguer Parlement of Provence had negotiated the submission of the province to him: the Paris court flattered itself that its celebrated declaration in favour of the Salic law against foreign aspirants to the crown had preserved the dynasty.

The members of the parlements, recruited from the richest merchant or financier families, assumed a social status higher than the increasingly impoverished nobility of the sword. The venality of offices, and the impossibility of the government being able to repurchase them, were the best guarantees of their immovability. Thus, while the nobility and the clergy lost their rights and privileges, the magistrature continued to grow in authority along with the monarchy, which it had so strongly aided against feudal powers in the middle ages. But it was inevitable that a struggle should break out between the kings, who tended to develop the forces of absolutism, and the high officers of justice, who, while they were zealous enough as servants of the crown, were attached to traditions, laws and their own privileges. As we have seen, the religious question had aggravated this discord, and the parlements had been involved in the general revolt.

. . . Most of the magistrates continued to charge a very high price for justice, when they did not actually sell it. . . . The financial officials deserved similar reproaches. . . . The disorganisation caused by the civil wars had impaired administration and officials of every grade had profited widely from the lack of control. No one knew any longer the precise details of taxes and resources. The state had even borrowed from its own financial officials, and since it was unable to pay both capital and interest, it closed its eyes to corruption and inefficiency. From top to bottom the financial administration practised a form of theft, and suffered still more from sheer disorder.

One of the gravest problems confronting Henry IV was the fact that the monarchy had ceased to be obeyed and respected. In the sixteenth century, as in other periods of crisis, the Estates General had asserted a right to intervene in the processes of government. Furthermore, Catholic France had broken with Henry III, refused to recognise Henry IV, and sought to abolish the Salic Law. Henry IV was clearly determined never to convoke the Estates, though he dared not say so. In a letter summoning an Assembly of Notables (July 28th 1596) he explained that he would have received the advice of his subjects "in a full assembly of the Estates General of this kingdom, had the armies and endeavours of our enemies allowed time to defer the need to provide for and remedy the evils that so closely beset us," and he also promised to convoke them a little later.

During the period of civil war the towns had resumed the right to administer themselves and to choose their consuls, mayors and councillors. They had levied their own taxes, with or without Mayenne's consent. They had expelled the commanders, governors and bishops who had given them offence. They had corresponded with foreign powers. After their submission to Henry IV, they had assumed that they would continue to control their municipal elections. Moreover, former Leaguers entrenched in the municipalities were able to exclude sound royalists from local government for a considerable period by making use of the general right possessed by the outgoing magistrates to exercise a controlling influence over the nomination of their successors. The *capitouls* retiring from Toulouse in 1597 wished to arrange the election of their successors from "certain persons of low estate, who lacked property and good name, were given to extreme mutiny and faction, and had shown themselves during the late disturbances to be fierce enemies of the King's service." With leaders such as these, those towns where the King had granted the right of self-defence, and where no royal citadels or garrisons were established, could serve as bases for a rebellion.

There was much discontent throughout the kingdom. Taxes were as heavy as they had been in the civil wars. The most just measures of government seemed tyrannical to some. The King had ordered that the *taille* should be imposed upon officers and soldiers who were not of noble rank, or who were no longer in service and had served less than twenty years, and this edict had applied to the cavalry [*gendarmes d'ordonnance*] and also the infantry captains, lieutenants and ensigns. There was bitter humiliation for those who believed themselves ennobled through military service, and those who had been of noble rank but whose titles had been lost in the disorder of the last of the wars. The memorialist Villegomblain, one of the malcontents, recorded that their claims were not well received by the King, "although some were wounded and disabled in his service, and others had contributed most of their property to his cause." Of the commissaries charged with the revision of the list of those exempted from the *taille*, "some through favour or money or the invention of their clerks very often exempted those who were by no means noble." To all the protestations against the excesses and abuses of these commissaries, which, according to Villegomblain, comprised the "most refined chicanery in France," the King said that he was unwilling "to break ordinances designed principally for the relief of his people," and so it "became necessary for most of those who wanted to avoid ruin to seek the ear of some minor treasury official."

Yet whether they were obliging or not, whether honest or corrupt, all these royal officials were equally detested by the nobility of the sword. Robert Dallington, who was secretary to the English embassy, expressed in his *View of France* (composed in 1598) an opinion that must have been felt more emphatically by the nobility: "It is a lamentable case, or at least misbeseeming, in a goodly country and full of nobility, that the state should be governed and all matters managed by them of the *robba longa,* advocates and procureurs and pen and inkhorn gentlemen."

The great were exasperated at the reduction of their hold on high office and feared it might soon become worse for them. Protestants, who had supported the King in his early campaigns, and Catholics, who had rallied to him at the death of Henry III, had served him in the field and known him with a familiarity born of common danger, military brotherhood and an uncertainty of what the future would bring. They were surprised to see the man they had known as a companion speak and act as though he were master, and they accused him of forgetting that he owed his crown to them. Perhaps they believed that he wished to make himself so powerful that "he could without any risk destroy or pull down all the great throughout the kingdom so that he might afterwards reign over the rest entirely as his whims suggested." The monarchy's claim must have seemed all the more strange to them since during the preceding half century the various parties had disputed the right of the crown to command by virtue of its possession of the sovereignty.

Protestant theorists had agreed in asserting that the monarchy was limited by the powers of the princes of the blood, or of established authorities, or of the Estates General. In the manner of Théodore de Bèze's *Authority of Magistrates over Their Subjects* (1574), but with greater fullness, the author of the *Vindiciae contra Tyrannos* (*A Defence of Liberty against Tyrants,* 1579—possibly by Du Plessis-Mornay) justified resistance to oppression. Subjects, he wrote, were not obliged to obey, and were even required to oppose by force anyone, be he usurper or legitimate prince, who oppressed the church or the state. Everyone had the right of legitimate defence against a usurper until he had been recognised as the ruler by the nation. It was permissible to fight against him and even to kill him. Within this last category of tyrants were included "those who tyrannise subjects through the stupidity or the indifference of the prince." Where it was a legitimate prince who behaved as a tyrant, however, it was necessary to act gently at first through advice and remonstrance, and recourse to arms was permitted only in the last resort. Moreover, it was for the great (the "inferior magistrates") to take action and to punish the tyrant. Individual men had no such right. Impostors who designed the role of Jehu for themselves were to be distrusted.

Catholic theorists went much further. When Boucher glorified the assassination of Henry III, he asserted that individual men might slay a tyrant, whereas the *Vindiciae contra Tyrannos* only allowed those chosen by God or the people to commit tyrannicide. The anonymous author of *De Justa Reipublicae Christianae in reges impios et hereticos authoritate* (*Concerning the Just Authority of a Christian Commonwealth against Impious and Heretical Kings*—1590), who was a typical representative of Leaguer propagandists, called for the assassination of the heretical Henry IV.

The theorists claimed that sovereignty resided in the people and that the power of the ruler was merely a delegation. The nation could depose the king, as it could place in tutelage a king who was incapable or insane. Regicide — the murder of a worthy king — was detestable, but tyrannicide was laudable. Even the humblest members of society might win "eternal glory and renown" by the slaughter of kings who acted tyrannically or ruled without proper title. Jacques Clément, the killer of Henry III, was described as "a most virtuous and illustrious young man" and his deed was called "a divine and heroic act."

Moreover, above and beyond the authority of the people existed the Church. The state had been constituted to allow the citizens to live in peace, to secure them in the ownership of property and to make possible the worship of God, in which the vital element was that of sacrifice. Christ had placed two magistrates at the head of his eternal church: that of the episcopacy and that of the monarch. The former was charged with spiritual responsibilities; the latter was subordinate to it and responsible for temporal affairs. The principal duty of kings had always been to employ the sword and the law to execute decisions made by bishops and councils of the church. When princes betrayed this duty they became tyrants and deserved to be treated as such.

Nothing survived of the democratic doctrines of the League. Ultramontane Catholics forgot the claims for the rights of the people, but they continued to maintain that the Pope had jurisdiction over kings. The doctrine of absolute monarchy came into conflict with papal supremacy, not popular sovereignty. Boucher's book and the *De Justa — Authoritate* had actually been preceded and were certainly followed by solid treatises representing the papacy as the sole sovereign power. Bellarmine, the great Jesuit theologian, had maintained as early as 1586 in his *Controversies* (*Disputationes de controversiis Fidei*) that the Pope could intervene in the internal affairs of kingdoms, and could abolish old laws, promulgate new ones and depose unworthy rulers. However, he made it clear that this right should only be used in the last resort when the safety of the Church was endangered. Ordinarily the Pope's responsibility was entirely spiritual, and his actions were restricted to the government of souls. In short, Bellarmine distinguished between the direct power of the Pope in spiritual matters and his indirect power in temporal affairs. The Index condemned the theory of indirect power as too restrictive, because it gave the Pope supreme authority — and only accidentally at that — when religion and the church were in grave danger. Papal pretensions had been confirmed by the support the popes had given the League and by the exclusion of the Protestant claimant to the throne despite dynastic right. Henry IV had only partially won his throne by conquest: he had also had to accept conversion to Catholicism to become truly King of France.

Gallicanism had been weakened in two respects: politically, in its claim for the independence of the crown from the Church, and, in terms of religious dogma, in its view that general councils of the Church were superior to popes. In face of the Protestant threat, the upper clergy had sought to live in close harmony with the Holy See. In the same sense the Faculty of Theology in Paris had accepted the supremacy of Rome. Even during the League, and afterwards until 1600, theses had been presented at the Sorbonne which maintained the traditional doctrine of the superiority of councils over popes. But after 1600 all supported the absolute power of St. Peter and his successors over the Church. Where former Leaguers were in a majority, the Parlements themselves adopted this view. This was not the situation in Paris, where the Parlement, alarmed by the attempt of Jean Châtel to murder Henry IV, had banished the Jesuits, who were the unwavering defenders of papal theocracy. At Toulouse and Bordeaux, however, the Jesuits were welcomed by the Parlements. The King himself made it his principal aim to remain on good terms with Rome.

Since ultramontane doctrines were so contrary to the traditions of the French church and the French monarchy, there was an inevitable reaction. Edmond Richer, a doctor of theology in the University of Paris read and recommended the reading of Gerson and the other great Gallican theorists of the fifteenth century. In 1594 Pierre Pithou, attorney-general at the Parlement, formulated the Gallican doctrine on relations between Church and state in his treatise *The Liberties of the Gallican Church,* which was to remain the catechism of political Gallicanism as long as there were Gallicans in France. Not only did it deny the Pope any temporal power, but it even limited his authority in the spiritual sphere by holding that he was restricted by canon law and by the decrees and customs of the Gallican church. Yet there were twenty-two bishops who denounced the book as heretical, and many minds remained disturbed and agitated by the disagreement between the spiritual and temporal authorities.

The assassins Barrière and Châtel had many imitators. All classes of society—priests, monks, women, soldiers, nobility—provided would-be instruments of tyrannicide. Some plotted to kill Henry IV with knife or dagger, others to shoot him down with an arbalest. Nicole Mignon, the tenant of the Stag's Horn Inn at Saint-Denis, offered to arrange to poison him for the comte de Soissons, and Richard, sieur de La Volte, made a similar offer to the Duke of Savoy. Saint-Germain, a member of the Norman nobility, together with a surgeon, even attempted to smother him. In the twelve years of peace, there were at least twelve attempts against his life.

This was the state of poverty, discontent and disorganisation in which France found herself in 1598. It fell to Henry IV to re-establish authority in Government, prosperity in the countryside and tranquillity in the minds of his subjects.

The Uprooting of the Nobility

PIERRE DE VAISSIÈRE

Pierre de Vaissière was a qualified archivist-paleographer, a graduate in law and a doctor of letters. He was a much-respected custodian of the French National Archives who specialized in sixteenth-century history. Among his publications, for which he was awarded several prizes by the French Academy and the Institute, were biographies of the ambassador Charles de Marillac, the Huguenot Guerilla leader Baron des Adrets, and Henry IV. He also wrote a study of the family of Joyeuse. His *Gentilshommes campagnards*, from which the following passage is excerpted, advanced a controversial thesis with color and verve at a time when research into the economic fortunes of the nobility of sixteenth-century France lacked the refined techniques of modern economic and demographic history. He argues that economic changes began a process, accelerated by the Wars of Religion, whereby the ancient aristocracy was uprooted from its hereditary lands. This thesis is employed as a key to explain the subsequent subjugation of the nobility by the Crown in the seventeenth century.

Towards the end of the fifteenth century France possessed a nobility which was detached from its feudal origins, and as yet betrayed no sign of its future decline. It is true that this nobility was deprived of the power it had once exercised, but it knew how to retain both its social influence and the moral authority that some historians would deny it. As a social group it remained in close contact with the lower classes. By its interests, its way of life and its customs it conformed perfectly to the aristocratic ideal in its worthiest sense. This part of our history forms a golden age for the nobility, though one that is too often overlooked. It extends from the end of the fifteenth century to the later years of the sixteenth, from the beginning of the Renaissance to the Wars of Religion. Study of the conditions of life, the social status and the daily habits of the privileged classes in this period should prove that the French nobility could successfully stand comparison with that English gentry with which it is often so unfavourably contrasted. . . . What, one might ask, was the distinctive characteristic of this aristocracy? What was its most striking and remarkable aspect? It was that it comprised a pre-eminently rural nobility, a nobility living from and on the land. So widespread was this way of life that when I write of the country gentleman I may confidently claim that I am speaking of the entire noble class at this time.

. . . It is precisely at this moment of equilibrium — at this point of balance created in sixteenth century France between the extreme particularism of the Middle Ages and the absolutism of the last phases of the monarchy — that the nobility of Francis I and Henry II assumed its distinctive characteristics. It was entirely devoted to the crown, which thenceforth could rely on its loyalty; but on the other hand, it displayed three intrinsic tendencies which connected it with the preceding age. These tendencies proclaimed its independent nature and distinguished it from the servile, domesticated aristocracy of the absolute monarchy of later years. First, it was an aristocracy deeply rooted in its native soil, whence it drew a robust vitality

From Pierre de Vaissière, *Gentilshommes campagnards de l'Ancienne France* (Paris, 1903), pp. 2–3, 8–9, 36–37, 215–224, 260. Reprinted by permission of Albin Michel. [Editor's translation.]

and a healthy vigour. Secondly, it remained a warrior class, constituting almost the entire national army and keeping its liberty and independence in the shifting military organisation of the time. Finally, a gentleman was not then just a soldier and defender of his country. The crown recognised the other rights of the nobility, and imposed upon it other duties. In concert with the crown's officials, or simply under their control, it assured the existence of order, dispensed justice, saw to the execution of the law, and took the initiative in parish affairs. Thus it placed itself at the service of the nation with devotion to society at large and respect for individual liberty in particular. It performed this role through the strength of its sword and the authority of its local influence. The manner in which it did so proved worthy of the rank it held.

. . . Many historians, and many eminent ones at that, date the decline of the French nobility from the sixteenth century. One of the first of the explanations they provide is the almost universal poverty of the aristocracy at this time. From the start of the sixteenth century is commonly dated the material ruin of a class which had previously owed much of its influence to its wealth.

I have already remarked on the falsity and exaggeration of a theory which, making play with a long evolutionary process, declares that at the very time when the French nobility emerged from the Middle Ages — at a time which ought to be termed its golden age — its role was ended. Those who support this view see the nobility in the light of seventeenth and eighteenth century documents, and consequently they do not hesitate to place its decline at least half a century too early. The alleged impoverishment of the aristocracy at the beginning of the sixteenth century is merely a point of detail supporting the general hypothesis.

This argument does not, I must confess, persuade me to withdraw my general criticism. If, indeed, the ruin of the majority of the French nobility can properly be placed in the last years of the sixteenth century, the process of decline cannot also be fixed at the earlier date. On the contrary, everything shows that the first half of the century was an era of exceptional prosperity for the nobility.

The first and possibly most decisive reason for this was the attachment of the nobility to its native soil. It makes good sense to say that this wealth and prosperity came essentially from the land. During the first half of the sixteenth century the fortune of the aristocracy remained essentially a landed one, as it had been, and, moreover, as it was to continue to be. At no other period was the political and economic condition of the country, as well as the practices of economy and order on the part of the landed proprietors, more favourable to the strong revival of agriculture. Nor was there a more astonishing increase than that which occurred in the value of land and in the revenues derived from it.

* * *

I shall now try to survey the historical, economic, moral and political causes of the uprooting of the French aristocracy at the end of the sixteenth century and throughout the seventeenth century. The historical causes must be taken first, not because they are the most important but because they are the most immediate. They are directly connected with the civil wars of the sixteenth century. The results of the religious conflicts have been considered from many standpoints, but there has possibly not been enough stress placed upon their social consequences. For the nobility these consequences were considerable. Continued recourse to arms in some provinces such as Guyenne lured the country gentlemen away from their estates, distracted them from the daily care of their lands, and gave them a taste for a wandering, vagabond life in place of the peaceful habits of former times. Yet this was only half the trouble, for at least these country gentlemen often remained in their own province. The court took a clear stand against Protestantism early in the conflicts, and for Catholics it quickly became a rallying point. For the Huguenots, on the other hand, the court was a citadel to be captured and an enemy to be fought. Thus both parties were moved for very different reasons to turn to the government — either to defend it or to attack it. In this way there occurred during the religious wars a kind of movement towards the throne that contributed in some fashion to political centralisation. On every occasion the provincial governors "sent messengers to the seigneurs within their jurisdiction, bidding them march with all speed to the aid of the King," and telling them, as Monluc told the Gascon nobility,

> what a joy it would be to His Majesty, to see his nobility coming to sustain him from the utmost parts of his kingdom, and that he would never forget such a service and would know how to reward it.

The same Monluc began to scoff at those gentlemen who "however poor they might be" would not leave "the pleasures of their homes, their wives and their dogs," and who, if they went to war, did so regretfully, "yearning always to return to their families and, like the franc-archer, only being prepared to fire their arquebuses when there was no other way of avoiding death." On their side the Protestant leaders drew the same support from the provinces and rallied about them veritable armies of country nobility, who were always ready to respond to the first call to arms with their numerical strength and their fighting prowess. As the Venetian ambassador, Pietro Duodo, tactfully put it, whether by their own choice or by necessity they were all ready to contribute to the success of their cause, regardless of the time or the place where they were actually required to gather to defend it. Unquestionably many of these partisans returned to their lands at every interval of peace; but there were also many who remained to throng the streets of Paris and the corridors and antechambers of the Louvre. There they formed escorts for their leaders, or claimed from the king rewards for their services, thus beginning their apprenticeship as courtiers. Under the League this tendency continued right to the end of the century. When Henry IV was proclaimed King of France he had still to conquer his kingdom. It was in large part due to the support of his loyal provincial nobility that he succeeded in doing so. He wrote to the "heads of the nobility of Périgord" commanding them "to gather together and leave their homes to join him, and so serve him as the occasion might demand": he summoned to him "his faithful nobility" from Ile-de-France, Beauce, Champagne, and Brie: he obliged Tavannes, his governor in Burgundy, to assemble the nobility of the province and march them to his aid without delay: he wrote to d'Humières, his lieutenant general in Picardy to lead his "good and devoted servants"; to Noailles, his governor in Auvergne, to send him all those who "wished to serve him." Moreover, his orders were fully obeyed. It is significant that towards the end of the war he began to consider it necessary to return to their homes "for purposes of rest and refreshment" all those gentlemen who crowded about him. They were difficult to persuade, and it was only by a clear and imperious order that he secured obedience. As his historian, Péréfixe, tells us, it was necessary to thin out from the ranks of his army many who crowded his court with importunate demands and requests.

These noble beggars of favours were not all, as one might think, men of ambition searching for advancement. There were many who saw in royal generosity and favour the only means of reestablishing their shattered fortunes or, at least, of postponing the threat of bankruptcy. In fact the wars of religion did not merely entail the general disorganisation of rural life and the consequent breaking of those bonds that had previously kept the country nobility on their estates: their economic effects were even more disastrous for the nobility. It is essentially from the religious wars that the impoverishment of the French nobility should be dated. This impoverishment placed the aristocracy at the mercy of the crown, and reduced it to a state of utter servitude.

. . . For the most part the men of the sixteenth century were blind to the economic revolution occurring in their midst. . . . The abundance of "fine and good" money, as Brantôme called it, was not, as he thought, a sign of prosperity but precisely the cause of that extraordinary depreciation of money which in France attained its maximum during the civil wars. . . . The placing in circulation of a so-called "infinity of treasure" by the French nobility was far from being a sign of the restoration of aristocratic fortunes. On the contrary, it was the most certain indication of impending poverty. A sudden increase in expenditure does not always imply the existence of immediate resources: more often it demonstrates a state of financial disaster. So it was for the nobility at the end of the sixteenth century. Whence, in actual fact, came these sums of money that allowed the nobility to put so bold a face on affairs? Generally, alas!, they were derived from the alienation of their domains, and from borrowing on mortgages. Forced borrowings and forced sales were the two gravest devices through which the material ruin of the aristocracy was consummated. . . . Those who acquired their domains were merchants, men of the law—bourgeois and new men from families recently enriched through commerce and business.

. . . Prodigality was not, as is often claimed, the only reason for the impoverishment of the aristocracy. In reality life had been hard and expensive for the nobility in this period of the civil wars, and their ruin was not due just to their mismanagement of their affairs. At every renewal of hostilities it had been necessary for them to equip themselves for war, and a great many had firmly refused to serve in the companies of men-at-arms because of the high cost of weapons and horses. Even in the infantry the continual campaigning weighed heavily on the purse of many. Add to this the expenses of long journeys, of the maintenance of garrisons and the daily temptations to which these men were exposed during their absence from their homes, and it will easily be seen that their new way of life could not be paid for from the revenues of their fiefs. Moreover, what had become of these revenues? I am not here concerned with the diminution in rent caused by the continued absence of a seigneur, who, far from his lands, could no longer supervise their exploitation in the customary way. Moreover he could not prevent bands of soldiery from destroying the crops of his peasantry, from seizing their livestock and burning their dwellings. I have not retraced here the details of the ravages in the countryside during the religious wars. I should like to make this simple point: that if one is always ready in such circumstances to pity the lot of the rural classes, the fact that the owners suffered as much from the devastation of the countryside as did the peasants may too easily be overlooked.

. . . From the beginning of the seventeenth century the French nobility moved progressively away from its origins, and every day it lost something more of that landed and rural character which had previously been its distinctive mark. It went on dividing itself ever more deeply into two classes, of which one prospered increasingly at the expense of the other. On the one hand, the nobility of the court, the army and of public office pursued those pensions, honours and dignities with which the royal power was always only too willing to satisfy its greed: on the other hand, the country nobility vegetated dismally in provincial obscurity.

The Hardening of Class Divisions

HENRI DROUOT

Henri Drouot (1886–1955) devoted his life to the history of his native province of Burgundy. He was a professor in the Faculty of Letters at the University of Dijon, and director of the journal *Annales de Bourgogne* from 1929 until his death. His massive study of the League in Burgundy was published in 1937, after presentation for his doctorate. In this work Drouot skillfully blends his account of economic and social changes with his narrative of political events. His principal concern is the strength of provincial separatism, but the paradox of a situation where Mayenne was both national leader of the League and independent ruler of Burgundy allows him to generalize more widely about the role of the great aristocracy in the period.

In this particular extract, however, Drouot discusses the economic and social changes accompanying the final phases of the Wars of Religion. He regards these changes as having a determining effect, and concludes that this period was marked by the replacement of social mobility with class barriers, and by the growth of class antipathies.

Among the holders of administrative and judicial office were some representatives of old noble families from the thirteenth and fourteenth centuries. In the face of the difficulties encountered in the fifteenth century some nobles had indulged in trade and, after regaining their wealth, had also regained their rank by means of offices — a path which had become more accessible after 1500 and which was esteemed to be honourable even by so exacting a member of the old nobility as Tavannes. It was not unusual to find presidents and judges of noble origin in the parlement at Dijon and in the administrative courts of the bailiwicks.

Now that these descendants of the men of the sword of former times rubbed shoulders in the financial and judicial courts not only with the sons or grandsons of merchants but also with the descendants of artisans and labourers who now had their own coats of arms. . . . Moreover there were no social barriers between these sons of merchants and the merchants themselves, nor between the top rank of provincial society and those lower classes on the land, whom they dominated and from whom they were derived. Intermediary groups provided the links in an articulated society. Apart from the privileges that accompanied ennoblement, wealth was then the true basis of social hierarchies. Although trade had been forbidden to the nobility from the middle of the century, it was not yet regarded as a handicap, and even such high places as the provincial sovereign courts, where diverse elements were fused together, still appeared accessible to any wealthy provincial. Money opened the door to every kind of social status.

This, at least, was the state of affairs in the middle of the sixteenth century, but thenceforth times began to change. The period before 1560 was one of material prosperity, in which many industrious persons had rapidly gathered together a fortune and risen to social prominence. From the rope-makers of Autun had emerged Jeanin, the future president of the Parlement, and, twenty-five leagues to the east, a family of blacksmiths and petty bourgeois

From Henri Drouot, *Mayenne et la Bourgogne: Etude sur la Ligue (1587–1596)* (Paris, 1937), vol. I, pp. 32–53. Reprinted by permission of Editions A. and J. Picard and Cie. [Editor's translation.]

at Ornans had thrust forward the future Nicolas Perrenot de Granvelle, Keeper of the Seals to the Emperor Charles V and himself the father of the great Cardinal Granvelle. By 1587, however, things were very different. Social ascensions had ceased with the economic and monetary crisis, and with the permanent replacement of foreign war and internal peace by civil war. Classes were more clearly defined. Most important of all, new social antagonisms arose and existing antipathies deepened. Religion might dress up these antagonisms in its own colours or strengthen them with fanaticism, but it was these class hatreds that served as the basis of local conflicts at the time of the League.

The general crisis of the nobility during the religious wars is a recognised fact, but it is not always recognised that it is a fundamental fact from which many consequences follow. It will be shown that the state of Burgundian society corresponds with the general situation. In the absence of precise statistics it appears from the abundance of noble names that the Italian and German wars had decapitated the old families without destroying their offshoots. While there were only a few great barons (the counts and viscounts de Saulx-Tavannes, the Chabot family bearing the titles of compte de Charny, baron de Brion and marquis de Mirebeau, and the Bauffremont, who were barons de Senneceyard and comtes de Cruzille), there was a multitude of simple gentlemen or squires. The numerical strength of the lower nobility constitutes an important aspect of the whole society. Another aspect immediately comes to notice — the decline in wealth of the great majority of these gentlemen of the sword. If the leading "barons" kept up the appearance of prosperity, a contrasting poverty was increasing among most of the nobility of lesser rank. Many examples, some of them dramatic, might be cited of this economic decline. When Claude de Villers died at Autun in December 1571, he left a burden of heavy debts to his six children, with houses in ruin and seigneuries in disarray. Then, very suddenly, their liabilities increased with borrowing and the alienation of their land. The widowed mother tried to avoid ruin by giving half her property to her eldest son. The second son entered the clergy and surrendered his inherited rights. A daughter was married without dowry. But it was all in vain. In 1584, at the death of the widow, Jeanne de Montjeu, twenty-two creditors claimed their due, and when the royal sergeant presented himself at the château de Montjeu to recover a single small debt, he found no furniture there worth the sum owing. Beside these cases of tragic ruin, there were more ordinary instances of slow decline: that of the Pontailler family, for example, which, continuing the decay experienced by the elder generation, was obliged continually to alienate small pieces of their lands in the years before 1588, and to eat into the lands reserved for their personal exploitation by alienating it as copyhold. Subsequently there occurred multiple borrowings on the security of their land. There were many other noble families exhibiting similar signs of their distress. Despite various measures of self-defence and an increasing number of civil suits heard by the courts of the bailiwicks, there was a growing number of decrees of forfeiture of "lands and seigneuries" after 1575 which demonstrated dramatically the plight of this class. It is difficult to know whether the Burgundian nobility suffered to the extent estimated by the Huguenot leader François de la Noue in 1587, when he asserted that throughout the kingdom eight out of every ten families were in such difficulties that they were obliged to alienate property. In any case, they endured that common fate of which the most alarming aspects had been revealed to them by beggared gentry migrating from the west, and of which the general trend had been indicated by the complaints of the order of the nobility at the Estates General of 1576.

Like the actual shortage of money, the underlying monetary, economic and social causes were evident in Burgundy. The

Burgundians were, for example, fully aware of the fashions brought from Italy, the demands of military extravagance, and the free mode of living fostered by a century of war. Large sums of money were squandered in building. The invasion of Italian architecture and ornamentation spread throughout the province. . . . These feverish extravagances . . . were as important a cause of the ruin of the nobility in Burgundy as they were elsewhere in France.

Beneath this extravagant attitude there often lay a very acute feeling that the status of the family had to be maintained. "High and puissant seigneur" was the usual formula employed in notarial transactions concerning the fortune of the smallest baron, and it scarcely permitted doubt as to the reality of family tradition. Yet there might well be doubt as to whether the resources of the seigneuries were adequate for these "puissant seigneurs."

. . . The general rights, quit-rents, revenues in kind, labour dues and rights of justice that comprised the seigneuries were infinitely diverse, and often varied from village to village within the same seigneuries, which at times were jointly owned by several seigneurs. The same diversity existed in the relative proportions of the seigneurial reserves and the lands occupied by tenants. Yet generally the records reveal that the reserve was of slight importance — a few fields besides the manor, a garden, some forest areas bearing rights of common usage and lands which were too far off or too poor to be cultivated or tenanted. The remainder was shared out in holdings, many of them extremely small.

The reserve, whether it was personally exploited by the seigneur or put out either at rent or under share-cropping arrangement, was the only really productive part of seigneurial property. The rest of a seigneurie only brought in services and mediocre dues. The reserve had to feed the seigneur's horses and provide his wine, his bread and his game. Labour dues had to provide for cultivation, cartage and care of the vineyards. But in actual fact the medieval labour dues had often been converted into money dues, which, like the quit-rents, had been devalued and no longer represented the true cost of their labour equivalent. To maintain the revenue from the reserve it was therefore necessary to depend upon free labour. . . . Another problem was that of alienation to leasehold. The Burgundian seigneur was absent through service in war, and leased out part of his reserve to labourers, according to the pattern throughout France. The seigneur's agent, who was a local man, either a small notary or merely a tenant bearing the office of sergeant, often put his own interests before that of his master . . . Then, to assure himself of a more certain, though a smaller, revenue, the owner agreed to the conversion of temporary leases to long term ones at lower rates.

. . . The lands in the hands of the nobility were devalued, and the civil war incessantly imposed new losses or new expenses. . . . To avoid disaster the nobleman sometimes took personal care of his affairs and tried to create new revenues. The Chabots themselves sold grain and made considerable profits. But more often than not patience and business sense were lacking in these men of the sword. They preferred to rely on royal favour and sought the intervention of a patron to secure some benefice for one of their sons, and some title at court for themselves — that, for instance, of ordinary gentleman of the household procured by the marquis de Ragny, the barons de Lux and de Cypierre, and Jacques de la Guiche, sieur de Sivignon, or that of squire to the king, obtained for the young Héliodore de Tyard, the nephew and protégé of the bishop and poet Pontus de Tyard. In this, however, fortune was reserved for a few, those who might be said to have been "presented" at court. The pensions and gifts of the king allowed some momentary crisis to be surmounted, but, subsequently, life at court proved expensive and the new income was apt to be paid in a very irregular fashion. Marriage with some daughter of a high bourgeois family of the robe, which had been ennobled or re-ennobled, or even marriage into some non-noble fortune, was another measure for which the nobility of the sword displayed no repugnance.

. . . But the most common resource was war. War, which precipitated the decline of the seigneurial domain, offered at the same time certain compensations. Towards the year 1587 service in the companies of ordnance or in temporary levies had become a common experience and a recognised career for the lesser nobility. One after another the great faction leaders, Condé, Coligny, the duc d'Alençon and the Guises, issued their summons for revolt and found their recruits in Burgundy. So, too, did the King himself. The profession of arms was the traditional calling of the poor nobility, but after 1563 the entire class had sought escape from their difficulties in war, and had adapted it to their needs. Former expeditions, those "voyages" into Italy where the Burgundians had followed Guise and Aumale, had hastened the ruin of many households and left behind them little else save a nostalgia for adventure. The barons who had proved themselves in these forays tried to draw more tangible profits from the civil wars. . . . For the Burgundian barons, as for so many members of the French nobility, this delight in war was a kind of revenge for the loss of their lands through the transactions registered by the notaries. They depended upon their swords for their defence against their social misfortunes, and for their day-to-day support.

As the old power based on the seigneurial domain had declined, urban capital had expanded in the hands of that social group where representatives of former noble families and of the merchant class intermingled. It was a class that was complex in its origins but homogeneous in its outlook — an outlook specifically that of the bourgeoisie. It concerned itself with methodical management, with productive marriage alliances, and with the consolidation of investments. This urban wealth found its principal aim and employment in the acquisition of land. . . . The bourgeois conquest of both seigneuries and non-noble lands had begun long before 1587. What the nobility of the sword lost, the bourgeoisie made their own. Moreover, by lending money to the peasant or providing him with stock on profitable terms, these bourgeois not only busied themselves with the extension of the role of urban capital in rural exploitation but they prepared to seize possession of the soil itself. . . . The principal beneficiaries of the transfer of rural property, in Burgundy as elsewhere, were the high officials of the sovereign courts. Little by little the passage of enfiefed property from the endebted nobility of the sword to the great nobility of the gown became the general trend near Dijon from the middle of the sixteenth century. The great "robins" also derived profit from the alienation of church property in 1587–1588, and especially from the alienation of the royal domain, a device of which increasing use was made by the monarchy since the time of Henry II. . . . Accession to seigneuries did not always precede accession to offices, but the latter were regarded as the essential mark of the rise in family status. While the genealogies register the multiplication of seigneuries held by the families of the judges of the Parlement and the fiscal court or *chambre des comptes,* they also give the impression that the wave of seigneurial acquisitions was closely linked with the possession of offices.

. . . Moreover a solidarity of sentiment about the protection of the noble status they had acquired came to dominate the entire upper society of the gown. At Dijon in the parishes of Saint-Médard, Saint-Michel and Saint-Jean, where the families of the great "robins" grouped themselves together, a network of protective marriage relationships was soon established, together with a feeling of common interests, expressed communally as a kind of class consciousness. There was a common awareness of the need to perpetuate the success they had achieved. Towards the year 1587 these "robins," who had upset the old social order during the preceding century, already composed a conservative group. They desired to maintain both the régime which had favoured their ascent and the peace which could guarantee their future. In this way they tended as a class to isolate themselves on the social summit to which they had climbed, and to draw up the ladder behind them.

. . . For forty years the number of advocates, attorneys, doctors, notaries and recorders had greatly increased within the social circle of small merchant families. In 1587 there was a large group of attorneys in Burgundy, as there was everywhere else in France. Their numbers had grown fivefold or more since 1500. They swarmed round the Parlement at Dijon, and round the lower courts in the small towns. These overflowing corporations of lawyers, this surplus of "legal chicaners," with their hunger to climb the social ladder, formed one of the essential elements in provincial society, and one, before all the others, to which it is necessary to turn to explain the composition of the groups which achieved political prominence in the period of the League.

. . . To the élite who led this turbulent middle class the venality of office in the sixteenth century had offered the opportunity of social success. The status of advocate was as highly reputed as that of judge and generally more popular. It could be exchanged for the latter at a price which many advocates, qualified for high office through their doctorates of law, could afford to pay. However, in 1587 the men of ambition among them no longer found open the path to the sovereign courts that had led the generation of 1550 to eminence.

While it developed its links with the nobility of the sword, the upper legal class appeared progressively to be shutting itself off from the advocates. By about 1580 in Burgundy the practice was current of resigning transmissible offices in favour of a son or a son-in-law. The former custom represented the anticipation of a patrimony by a son and the latter was a means of providing a dowry for a daughter. Letters of provision or the simple lists of officials afford clear evidence of this. An effective kind of heredity of office had been established in the interest of family connections. Offices were being transformed into family property, and the monarchy, which accepted this hereditary transmission with the tax of "the third penny" paid to the special treasury known as the *Parties casuelles,* had officially sanctioned the practice by the edicts of 1567 and 1568.

In the years 1580–1587 an important social consequence of this transformation became apparent in Burgundy. By creating and selling offices the monarchy under Francis I and Henry II had opened a way to social ambitions at the very time when economic prosperity provided able men with an easy means of entry to the upper levels of the provincial hierarchy. But under Henry III office-holders in Burgundy contrived to assert a firm control of their positions through the practice of hereditary transmission. They progressively forbad access to their posts to a crowd of graduates in law, who, like themselves, owed their claims to wealth that had been acquired in the period of internal peace. These newcomers found the path barred to situations reserved for the sons, sons-in-law, and nephews of the holders. The issue had certainly not yet arisen of the proud isolation of a privileged class that was to produce such momentous consequences in the eighteenth century: quite simply, it was a slowing down in the rate of absorption of a social group which continued to attract recruits while itself experiencing frustration. However many new offices were created, their number in the period of the League proved inadequate to compensate for the effects of the partial restriction. While the number of posts that might be purchased rapidly diminished, the flood of candidates doubled in volume and increased the pressure. The expansionist trend in personal fortunes slowly decreased after 1550 under the impact of the monetary and economic crisis. But another effect of this same crisis had been, after the beginning of the civil war, the diversion from business of the sons of merchants who had equipped themselves with doctorates of law with the intention of securing offices. The timing of this had important consequences. The barriers to advancement were erected at the very moment when these young doctors of law sought entry. The hitherto uncertain definition of social status seemed to have been fixed to their disadvantage by those who had reached the top of the ladder of bourgeois ascension.

When they found their path obstructed they made known their bitterness at their deception. In this respect these young lawyers resembled the artisans who discovered that the route to masterships in the Burgundian guilds was barred. These artisans freely expressed their resentments and became willing revolutionaries who turned to religious novelties, or to political activities influenced by new social forces. Similarly the advocates, finding the customary paths closed, sought new paths. While the aristocrats of the gown, strengthened by their material wealth and their governmental authority, depended upon the traditional monarchical régime, the ambitious troublemakers, whom the Bishop of Auxerre held to be "making themselves great by dreams and fantasies," seized onto the idea of another aristocracy, based upon the communes.

A Revolution in Land Ownership: The Expropriation of the Peasants

GEORGES LIVET

Georges Livet is Professor in the Faculty of Letters and Social Science and in the Institute of Political Studies at the University of Strasbourg. He has specialized in seventeenth-century Alsatian institutional history, and has an interest in the sociology of religion. Perhaps his best-known work is his study of the intendancy of Alsace in the reign of Louis XIV, which was published in 1956 and presented as his doctoral thesis. His short survey of the Wars of Religion, from which the ensuing extract is taken, makes use of a large number of recent specialized monographs on economic and social changes in sixteenth-century France which are not easily available to English-speaking students. He draws particular attention to the effects of the Wars of Religion on Church and peasant land ownership.

Two SETS of figures would be necessary to reveal the effects of the Wars of Religion upon the land problem: the first to show the destruction caused by the ravages of war; the other to show the consequences of the rise in prices in terms of personal fortunes. Each town and each region lived its own life, and any general conclusions for France as a whole in the sixteenth century must be treated with caution. Abstract terms such as the bourgeoisie and the nobility are often called into play where the truth concerns a myriad of individual destinies, in which suffering and

From Georges Livet, *Les Guerres de Religion* (Paris, 1962), pp. 90–97. Reprinted by permission of Presses Universitaires de France. [Editor's translation.]

secret heroism, fear, ambition and self-interest are all to be discerned. Recent studies have been devoted to the area round Paris, the head and heart of the conflict, to Burgundy and to the west and south of France. They suggest one general line of division among the participants in the long drawn out drama — that between those who suffer ruin and those who profit from the situation.

Within the first category are those fundamentally engaged in the struggle, namely the two main antagonists, the Catholic clergy and the persecuted Huguenots. The working hypotheses of the abbé Carrière in *Les épreuves de l'Eglise de France* [*The Ordeal of the Church of France*], which is in effect a new version of the "Discourse on the Miseries of this Time," must be systematically sifted. The clergy participated in the conflict in an active way. It was attacked not only through its members, its monasteries and its churches but also through the very principle of ownership — "remembering that the men of the Church are merely administrators and that they will render account for their stewardship." The Church was obliged to throw out some ballast. Various demands had to be met by multiple alienations of temporal property. These demands included the ordinary and extraordinary taxes on the church (*décimes*), temporary or conditional loans to the monarchy without interest, and the constitution of government stock. The alienations were effected under Charles IX and Henry III. They cut away half of the fixed capital of the Church, and cost it at least twenty million livres.

The alienation of Church property was a new idea, emanating from the Estates General of Orleans in 1561. There were six such instances, three under Charles IX and three under Henry III. The first, which was imposed on the Church on May 17th 1563, ordered the levying of a quarter of the fixed capital within those wealthy benefices of the kingdom that had paid the *décime* of 1516 to the amount of 100,000 livres, giving a total of about 3,200,000 livres. This was the most significant alienation, despite the edict ordering the repurchase of the property which was received by the clergy on January 7th 1564. The other alienations, which took place in 1568, 1568–1569, 1574, 1576 and 1586, were authorised by pontifical bulls. The history of the alienation of 1586 gives an idea of the great variety of the property sold, and of those who acquired it in the rich dioceses of northern France. It gives some impression, too, of the smallness of alienations made in central France, where account must be taken of the abundance of quit-rents and propertied annuities, as well as of the modest purchase prices paid by relatively poor members of the third estate. Equal attention must be given to alienations of judicial rights and of seigneuries in the southern dioceses, where purchasers from the nobility and upper bourgeoisie made important acquisitions, and where numerous beneficed clergy possessed sufficient revenue to pay their tax without recourse to the sale of property. Finally let us note that among the buyers there were, besides Huguenots such as the prince de Condé, certain leaders of the clergy who favoured their families and allowed them to obtain church property cheaply. Those who farmed the revenues of ecclesiastical communities profited equally from the occasion, but a great deal of research is still necessary before the importance of these land transfers can be known.

The Protestants suffered from edicts of proscription through their property if not through their persons. In every town the populace were ready to descend upon the goods of those whom the civil power handed over to them. Catholics themselves were not spared. The reservations expressed by certain governors to the orders given by the King after the massacre of St. Bartholomew may be seen in this light. In Paris the Papal nuncios bore witness: "The homes of the Huguenots have been broken into by the populace, who have shown an unbelievable greed. Such men will tonight spend much money on their horses, replace their coaches, and eat and drink from silver plate in a manner they have never dreamed of in all their lives." The delay of six months introduced by the edict of 1585 was reduced to three months and then to a fortnight. It involved the veritable legal dispossession of those Huguenots who lived in districts where they were in a minority. The royal commission sequestered their goods and sold some of them at nominal prices. In Flanders some well-to-do Huguenots had their property registered in the names of their children. In 1587 the complaint spread through Paris that the goods of the Huguenots had not been sold, and that Henry III ought publicly to set matters in motion. The same thing occurred under the League with the property of Politiques. At a time when a bridge had collapsed, the diarist L'Estoile, noting the death of several persons, added: "They were all rich people in easy circumstances, but their wealth came from usury and pillage at the time of St. Bartholomew and the League." It is interesting to speculate whether much of this stolen property was ever returned to its rightful owners, or, where they had disappeared, to their heirs.

Whence came the money used to purchase confiscated land? Those who were already wealthy and who, having profited from the inflation, were anxious to disembarass themselves of coin that might burn their fingers in this period of monetary instability, invested in land. It was a safe investment, even at a time when government stock appeared attractive or offices for sale increased rapidly in number. The first beneficiary was the nobility of the sword in the district of Gâtine, the nobility of the gown in the area round Paris. Thanks to the Parlement and to lower courts, the seigneurie exercised a controlling hand over arable land. It controlled debts, presided at the sale of communal property, and policed the parish dues. The seigneur at first lent money, then proceeded to buy, reunited to his domain property where title had lapsed, and developed share-cropping enterprises. The big share-cropping farm provided the best means for procuring a return on investments. In Gâtine within the province of Poitou its development changed the rural landscape. Through this means the seigneur, whether he was a nobleman or a bourgeois, profited from the high prices for grain and the reduction of the middling and small farmer to labouring status. He often escaped the *taille,* and its mounting total fell on the remainder of the parish. Of 175 contracts examined by P. Raveau in upper Poitou, 133 represented acquisitions by merchants, bourgeois and nobles, and 42 acquisitions by labourers. Changes took place in the ownership of feudal dues and also of entire seigneuries to the advantage of townsmen. Jehan Pocquelin, bourgeois of Beauvais, offers an example of a skilled profiteer in these matters. He acted as a merchant draper, an investor in land mortgages, a seller of wood and of grain, a pawnbroker, and also as a rural proprietor.

In the country three classes profited from the economic situation. First, the labourers who owned their land were in a position of advantage. They were already well-placed at the beginning of the century, and were described by notaries as "honourable persons." The possession of ploughing oxen and the labour provided by a numerous family allowed them to participate in new share-cropping. Secondly, those labourers who also dealt in merchandise were provided with ready cash by the sale of grain, wood and fodder. They set themselves up in business but they retained some land which they cultivated by employing day-labourers. Thirdly, those who farmed seigneuries were able to profit from the collection of *dîmes,* from the rights on wines and salts, and from local tolls. Thus the expansion of trade in primary produce remained within the hands of a minority. They profited from a certain stability in rents, from the depreciation of seigneurial dues paid in cash, and from farmlands that prospered by surviving where others had been destroyed. They slipped into that class of larger landowners, either seigneurs or bourgeois, who had transformed themselves from investors in landed rents to collectors of landed property.

The victims of these changes remained the small peasants, whose labour was exploited by all those who enriched themselves or speculated at their expense. Their life is recorded in the records of household inspections and notarial deeds, and in the writings of Noël du Fail and the chronicle of the Sire de Gouberville. In the vicinity of Paris these peasants are shown by the research of M. Jacquart to have lacked both reserves of capital and seed. They were obliged to buy part of their food, and they were crushed by the *tailles* and the demands of the leaders of war bands, as recorded by Blaise de Montluc. They lost first the means to work, their horses and cattle being requisitioned for feeding troops and military convoys. Indebted and overtaxed, rural communities sold their property, their woods and their pastures. The sale of private property followed a set pattern. The borrowing of money or grain from some profiteer would be followed by the constitution of mortgages on movables or land with heavy interest rates which in theory were repayable. Then came the sale of small parcels of property on the instructions of royal officers to pay off some outstanding debt. The only peasants who were in some degree protected from the activities of land speculators were those bound to the soil by *mainmort*. Serfdom provided a shield for peasant land, but, on the other hand, there was a perceptible trend towards enfranchisement. This was less a matter of natural law than it was a return to economic circulation of property previously unavailable in the land market. In the opinion of Saint-Jacob the great economic change of the century was the shift from the ideal of being master of one's own property to a desire to invest in *rentes,* farms, crops and commerce in general. The syncopated rhythm of the wars allowed economic life to draw breath, and permitted some to register sales, others to realise their gains and leave the countryside for the town. Those who were satisfied with their profits became the most ardent advocates of a lasting peace. Taine's view of the French Revolution as a wholesale transference of property may possibly be applied to the Wars of Religion.

There were many forms of peasant reaction to the devastations stigmatised by Ronsard in 1563 and the "legal spoliations" recorded in the local registers. They were demonstrated in a long series of popular disturbances, which had been numerous during the Hundred Years War and at the beginning of the sixteenth century. These varied from associations for common defence, which earned fear and respect, to the open *jacquerie* and its brutal repression. In Comminges, where official authority was weak, and also in Dauphiné leagues for mutual defence were organised. These came into direct conflict with the nobility. In Vivarais, where peasant organisation was not particularly advanced, a number of agreements regulating peasant labour were negotiated. Revolt remained the ultimate remedy, and in certain districts some conflicts became so much the rule that a genuine class consciousness appeared. In 1590 the provincial Estates of Burgundy resolved that "in the light of past experience and the inconveniences that may result, it will not be permitted for village communes to take up arms" even with the intention "of making war on the enemy." The bourgeoisie distrusted the arming of peasants. In Provence the brutal repression of 1545 and the alliance of the King and the Parlement of Aix did not resolve any of the lively antagonisms that existed in the social and religious spheres. Beza spoke of sixty Protestant churches in the province. The struggle involving the Provençal peasantry was centred round the Vaudois villages between the Durance River and the Lubéron Mountains. In Guyenne oral tradition passed on the memory of the revolt against the salt tax of 1548 and 1549. It had extended as far as Bordeaux despite the exhortations of the municipal authorities and the Parlement. The peasant *gauthiers* of Perche, who were crushed by the duc de Montpensier in April 1589 between Argentan and Falaise, were succeeded by the *francs museaux, chateauverts* or *lipans* between 1589 and 1593. Normandy even sent a peasant deputy to the Estates General of 1593. In Brittany the peasants did not hesitate to attack the towns held by Mercoeur, and the peasant movements of 1589 and 1590 were marked by attacks that were accompanied by liturgical singing. In the areas controlled by the League, these peasant revolts were directed against any army in the field, regardless of political party.

In Burgundy peasant uprisings continued as late as 1592. The peasants were involved in the awakening of the urban lower classes against the "preachers" and the "rich." In Beaunois and Châlonnais the peasants who cultivated the vineyards wore cuirasses and fortified themselves with earthworks. Many local movements, defensively organised at first, or in the form of associations of communes possessing militia, responded to the call of the tocsin. Their leaders were usually noblemen, but this was not often the case in Brittany where the soldiery was composed of petty gentry and parish clergy. There was even a pride in humility from the religious and social point of view. The malcontents of Meursault did not draw up articles in the style adopted by those in Lower Brittany. They did not claim "the right to marry women of noble stock, nor did they occupy châteaux and proclaim themselves seigneurs." They did not have behind them, like the peasantry of Trégorre, "a crowd of embittered lesser gentry." The Burgundian levy remained based on peasant landowners, notably the owners of vineyards, which in the Côte region compensated for the absence of the gentry. Isolated and lacking arms, this rural class stood aside in the years 1589–1593. In 1594, according to Henri Drouot, they wanted to enter the towns, to bring "freedom" to their inhabitants and to strike the final blow against Mayenne's regime.

Thus every peasant reaction presented its own original characteristics. In Burgundy it was conservative and in support of peace. In Brittany it showed strong social and anti-urban aspirations. In Limousin it was directed against the nobility and the taxation system, and its scope became very wide when the "*croquants*" succeeded in gathering 50,000 men to their standard. They extended from Limousin into Périgord, Quercy, Poitou and Saintonge and posed a major problem of public order. Henry IV wished to avoid the use of violence against them, but on 24th June 1593 the nobility attacked and massacred more than 2000 peasants. The siege of Gimel, whence the robber baron who commanded the fortress withdrew to Auvergne, allowed Jean de Thumery to pacify the area. On March 16th, 1595 the King abolished the arrears of the *taille,* and took the necessary measures to extinguish debts. This was not a sufficient palliative. Henry IV's attempts to restore peasant prosperity proved to be no more than a truce or a respite in peasant poverty. The Wars of Religion exacerbated or burst the abscesses of social discontent, but it is the ruin of the old agricultural system, accompanied by the expropriation of the peasantry, that explains in part the popular disturbances of the seventeenth century.

SUGGESTIONS FOR ADDITIONAL READING

A general guide to sixteenth-century sources is provided by Henri Hauser, *Les Sources de l'histoire de France au XVIe siècle* (vols. 3 and 4, Paris, 1912 and 1916). A bibliographical survey of secondary literature is contained in *"Clio," le XVIe siècle* by Henri Sée, Armand Rébillon and Edmond Préclin (Paris, 1950). The field is a vast one, especially in the area of local studies, but the number of books on the Wars of Religion published in English is relatively slight. From the period of the conflicts to our own day a large proportion of the relevant historical works have been partisan in character. Yet even in the age of the religious wars there were some writers, notably Jacques-Auguste de Thou and Enrico Davila, who displayed a judicious impartiality. The highly selective list that follows is generally limited to historians whose insights have not been obscured by their prejudices. Those marked by an asterisk are represented by extracts earlier in this volume.

General Histories

Established general histories of the period forming part of a larger series are those by Henri Hauser (*La Prépondérance espagnole** in *Peuples et Civilisations* edited by Halphen and Sagnac, Paris, 1934); J-H. Mariéjol (*La Réforme et la Lique* in *Histoire de France* edited Lavisse vol. VI, Paris 1911); Roland Mousnier (*Les XVIe et XVIIe siècles,* vol. V in *Histoire Générale des civilisations,* Paris 1961). Among other general surveys are those by Edward Armstrong (*The French Wars of Religion,* Oxford, 1904); Louis Batiffol (*The Century of the Renaissance,* London, 1927); A. J. Grant (*The French Monarchy,* vol. 1, Cambridge, 1900); Georges Livet (*Les Guerres de Religion,** Paris, 1962); J. E. Neale (*The Age of Catherine de Medici,** London, 1943); R. Stephan (*L'Epopée Huguenote,* Paris, 1945). An interesting selection of extracts from sixteenth-century sources has been published by Julien Coudy (*Les Guerres de Religion,* Paris, 1962). Translated selections from the *Journal* of Pierre de l'Estoile are provided by Nancy Roelker (*The Paris of Henry of Navarre,* Harvard, 1958).

International Aspects

The international aspects of the Wars of Religion have yet to be studied as a whole. Various elements in European diplomacy at the time are discussed by Louis Anquez (*Henri IV et l'Allemagne,* Paris, 1887); J. R. Black (*Elizabeth and Henry IV* Oxford, 1914); Fernand Braudel (*La Méditerranée et le Monde méditerranéen à l'époque de Philippe II,** Paris, 1949); Pierre Champion (*Charles IX, la France et le contrôle de l'Espagne,* 2 vols, Paris, 1939); E. Frémy (*Un ambassadeur libéral sous Charles IX et Henri III, Arnaud du Ferrier,* Paris, 1880); K. de Lettenhove (*Les Huguenots et les Gueux,* 6 vols., Bruges, 1883–1885); Garrett Mattingly (*Renaissance Diplomacy,* Boston, 1955, and *The Defeat of the Spanish Armada,* London, 1959); G. Baguenault de Puchesse (*La Politique de Philippe II dans les affaires de France 1559–1598* in *Revue des Questions historiques,* 1879); Félix Rocquain (*La France et Rome pendant les Guerres de Religion,* Paris, 1924). H. G. Koenigsberger has written a short comparative study of the Huguenots, the League and the resistance movement in the Netherlands ("The Organization of Revolutionary Parties in France and the Netherlands during the Sixteenth Century" in *Journal of Modern History,* XXVII, 4, 1955, pp. 335–351).

Religious Aspects

Some of the most complex religious problems of the period are discussed with sympathy and insight in the collected essays of Lucien Febvre, published as *Au Coeur religieux du XVIe siècle,* Paris, 1957.

Among general histories of French Protestantism are those by J. Chartrou-Charbonnel (*La Réforme et les Guerres de Religion,* Paris, 1936) and P. Imbart de la Tour (*Les Origines de la Réforme en France,* vols 3 and 4, Paris, 1914 and 1935). Protestant viewpoints are discernible in Jean Viénot (*Histoire de la Réforme française des origines á l'Edit de Nantes,* Paris, 1926), in the second volume of Emile Léonard's *Histoire générale du protestantisme* (*L'Etablissement,* Paris, 1961) and in Samuel Mours' *Le Protestantisme en France au XVIe siècle** (Paris, 1959 — especially valuable for its provincial studies of the Huguenot churches). Insights into the social attitudes of French Protestantism are provided by Hauser (*Etudes sur la Réforme,* Paris, 1909); Léonard (*Le Protestant français,* Paris, 1955); and André Biéler (*La Pensée économique et sociale de Calvin* Geneva, 1961). A view sympathetic to Calvin is presented in the massive work of Emile Doumergue (*Jean Calvin, les hommes et les choses de son temps,* 8 vols., Lausanne, 1899–1927). Robert M. Kingdon stresses the role of the Genevan pastors in France in *Geneva and the Coming of the Wars of Religion in France** (Geneva, 1956), and R. Nurnberger gives a general account of the nature of French Protestantism in *Die Politisierung des französischen Protestantismus* (Tubingen, 1948). For the history of Huguenot political assemblies see Louis Anquez (*Histoire générale des Assemblées politiques des Réformés en France, 1573–1622* (Paris, 1859). V. Carrière provides a general view of French Catholicism in the sixteenth century (*Les épreuves de l'Eglise de France au XVIe siècle,* Paris, 1936), while Louis Serbat discusses the financial affairs of the Gallican church and the support of the Catholic clergy for the introduction of the decrees of the Council of Trent (*Les Assemblées du clergé de France 1561–1615,* Paris, 1906). French Catholic participation in the Council of Trent is described by H. C. Evennett (*The Cardinal of Lorraine and the Council of Trent,* Cambridge, 1930).

Particular Phases

The origins of the Wars of Religion are discussed at length by Lucien Romier (*Les origines politiques des guerres de religion* 2 vols, Paris, 1913; *Le royaume de Catherine de Médicis,* 2 vols, Paris, 1922; and *Catholiques et Huguenots à la cour de Charles IX,* Paris, 1924). The conspiracy of Amboise has been examined by Romier (*La conjuration d'Amboise,* Paris, 1923), Henri Naef (*La conjuration d'Amboise et Genève,* Geneva, 1922), and L-R. Lefèvre (*Le Tumulte d'Amboise,* Paris, 1949). J. Russell Major has studied the Orleans Estates-General (*The Estates General of 1560,* Princeton, 1951). The period of Huguenot resistance is covered in detail by James Westfall Thompson (*The Wars of Religion in France, 1559–1576,** New York, 1909). Recent works on the Massacre of St. Bartholomew include those of Henri Noguères (*La Saint-Barthélemy,* Paris, 1959) and Philippe Erlanger (*Le Massacre de la Saint-Barthélemy,* Paris, 1960). General studies of the League are given by Maurice Wilkinson (*A History of the League or Sainte Union 1576–1595,* Glasgow, 1929) and Victor de Chalambert, (*Histoire de La Ligue,* Paris, 1898); while among particular studies are those of L. Davillé (*Les pretentions de Charles III, duc de Lorraine à la couronne de France,* Paris 1908); Henri Drouot (*Mayenne et la Bourgogne,** 2 vols, Paris, 1937); M. Bouard (*Sixte Quint, Henri IV et la Ligue,* Bordeaux, 1932); Paul Robiquet (*Paris et la Ligue sous le règne de Henri III,** Paris, 1886); De Lamar Jensen (*Diplomacy and Dogmatism — Bernadino de Mendoza and the French Catholic League,** Harvard, 1964). Corrado Vivanti (*Lotta politica e pace religiosa in Francia fra cinque e seicento,* Turin, 1963) presents a new view of Henry IV's policies towards the Protestant and Catholic churches at the end of the wars.

Biographical Studies

The period is rich in biographical studies, among which the following are particularly recommended: Le duc d'Aumale (*Histoire des princes de Condé pendant les XVIe et XVIIe siècles,* 7 vols, Paris, 1863–1896); Auguste Bailly (*Henri le Balafré, duc de Guise,* Paris, 1953); Henry M. Baird, *Theodore Beza,* New York, 1899); Albert Buisson (*Michel de l'Hospital,* Paris, 1950); Francis de Crue (*Anne, duc de Montmorency,* Paris, 1889); Charles Dufayard (*Le Connétable de Lesdiguières,* Paris, 1892); Philippe Erlanger (*Henri III,* Paris, 1948); Henri Forneron (*Les ducs de Guise et leur époque,* 2 vols Paris, 1877); A. Garnier (*Agrippe d'Aubigné et le parti protestant,* Paris, 1928); P. F. Geisendorf (*Theodore de Bèze,* Geneva, 1949); Henri Hauser (*François de la Noue,* Paris, 1892); Jean Héritier *Catherine de Médicis,** Paris, 1940); Jean-H. Mariéjol (*Catherine de Médicis,* Paris, 1920, and *La Vie de Marguerite de Valois,* Paris, 1928); Joseph Nouaillac (*Villeroy, secrétaire d'état et ministre de Charles IX, Henri III et Henri IV,* Paris, 1908); Franklin C. Palm (*Politics and Religion in Sixteenth-Century France. A study of the career of Henry of Montmorency-Damville, Uncrowned King of the South,* Boston, 1927); R. Patry (*Philippe du Plessis-Morney, 1549–1623,* 2 vols, Paris, 1933); Marcel Reinhard (*Henri IV ou la France sauvée* Paris, 1943); Edith Sichel (*The Later Years of Catherine de' Medici,* London, 1908); N. M. Sutherland (*Catherine de Medici and the Ancien Régime,* London, 1966); Paul van Dyke (*Catherine de Médicis* 2 vols, New York, 1922 and 1927); Pierre de Vaissière (*Messieurs de Joyeuse, 1560–1615,* Paris, 1926); A. W. Whitehead (*Gaspard de Coligny, Admiral of France,* London, 1904).

Economic and Social Change

Currency problems connected with the increased circulation of precious metal in sixteenth-century France are discussed at length by F. C. Spooner (*L'Economie mondiale et les frappes monétaires en France, 1493–1680,* Paris, 1956). The rise in prices is examined by Henri Hauser (*Recherches et documents sur l'histoire des prix en France de 1500 a 1800,* Paris, 1936); Micheline Baulant and Jean Meuvret (*Prix des céréales extraits de la Merciale de Paris, 1520–1620,* Paris, 1960 — the statistics are preferable to Hauser's figures); and André Liautey (*La Hausse des Prix et la Lutte contre la cherté en France au XVIe siècle,* Paris, 1921). Two important provincial studies of the consequences for the rural classes are by Henri Sée (*Les classes rurales en Bretagne du XVIe siècle à la Révolution,* Paris, 1906) and Paul Raveau (*L'agriculture et les classes paysannes: la transformation de la propriété dans le Haut-Poitou au XVIe siècle,* Paris, 1926). The effects of the price revolution upon urban as well as rural society are discussed in provincial setting by Henri Drouot in the work cited earlier. General views are presented by Braudel (already cited); Gustave Fagniez (*L'Economie sociale de la France sous Henri IV 1589–1610,* Paris, 1897); Marc Bloch (*Les caractères originaux de l'histoire rurale française,* 2 vols, Oslo 1931); Hauser (*Les débuts du capitalisme,* Paris, 1931). The rural nobility is the subject of particular studies by Pierre de Vaissière (*Gentilshommes compagnards et l'anciennce France,** Paris, 1925) and Henri Baudrillart (*Gentilshommes ruraux de la France,* Paris, n.d. [1893 ?] — discussing the contemporary accounts of sixteenth-century rural life by Gouberville, Noel du Fail and Olivier de Serres). Commercial changes are described by Pierre Jeannin (*Les Marchands au XVIe siècle,* Paris, 1957) and Henri Lapeyre (*Une famille de marchands, les Ruiz,* Paris, 1955). The expansion of credit is the subject of a study of private and public *rentes* by Bernard Schapper (*Les Rentes au XVIe siècle,* Paris, 1957). "Industrial" changes are discussed by John U. Nef (*Industry and Gov-*

ernment in France and England 1540–1640 [1940], New York, 1957). A work of synthesis is the study of sixteenth-century social attitudes by Robert Mandrou (*Introduction à la France moderne — essai de psychologie historique, 1500–1640,* Paris, 1961).

Institutions and Ideas

The most extensive modern work on French political institutions in the sixteenth century is that by Roger Doucet (*Les institutions de la France au XVIe siècle,* 2 vols, Paris, 1948). A smaller but equally valuable work is Gaston Zeller's book of the same title (Paris, 1948). For the Estates-General see Georges Picot (*Histoire des Etats Généraux, 1355–1614,* 4 vols, Paris, 1872) and J. Russell Major (*Representative Institutions in Renaissance France 1421–1550,* Wisconsin, 1960, and the work already cited). Edouard Maugis (*Histoire du Parlement de Paris de l'avènement des rois Valois à la mort d'Henri IV,* 2 vols, Paris, 1913) has written the authoritative work on the Parlement of Paris. The secretaries of state form the subject of a recent study by N. M. Sutherland (*The French Secretaries of State in the Age of Catherine de Medici,* London, 1962), and of an old work by Nouaillac (cited under biography). The sale and hereditary transmission of office is discussed in magisterial fashion by Roland Mousnier (*La Vénalité des offices sous Henri IV et Louis XIII,* Rouen, 1945).

The best general work in the history of ideas in the period is possibly that by Pierre Mesnard (*L'essor de la philosophie politique au XVIe siècle,* Paris, 1936). A survey of political literature, much wider in scope than its title suggests, is by Charles Lenient (*La satire en France, ou la littérature militante au XVIe siècle,* 2 vols, Paris, 1866). Lucien Febvre's *Le problème de l'incroyance au XVIe siècle — la religion de Rabelais* (Paris, 1942) has been widely acclaimed in its field. A most detailed discussion of Huguenot political thought in its early phases is provided by Vittorio de Caprariis (*Propaganda e pensiero politico in Francia durant le guerre de religione, 1559–1572,* Naples, 1959). Other books recommended are by J. W. Allen (*A History of Political Thought in the Sixteenth Century,* London, 1928); William Farr Church (*Constitutional Thought in Sixteenth Century France,* Harvard, 1941); Charles Labitte (*De la démocratic chez les prédicateurs de la Ligue,* Paris, 1865); Georges de Lagarde (*Recherches sur l'esprit politique de la Réforme,* Paris, 1926); André Lemaire (*Les lois fondamentales de la monarchie française d'après les théoriciens de l'Ancien Régime,* Paris, 1907); P. F. M. Méaly (*Les publicistes de la Réforme sous François II et Charles IX,* Dijon, 1903); Beatrice Reynolds (*Proponents of Limited Monarchy in Sixteenth Century France: Francis Hotman and Jean Bodin,* New York, 1931); J. H. M. Salmon, (*The French Religious Wars in English Political Thought,** Oxford, 1959); and Georges Weill (*Les théories sur le pouvoir royal en France pendant les Guerres de Religion,* Paris, 1892).

1 2 3 4 5 6 7 8 9 0